Selections from

HISTORY TODAY

General Editor

C. M. D. CROWDER

THE EXPANSION OF EUROPE

A Selection of Articles from *History Today*
with an original introductory essay by

JOHN D. HARGREAVES

OLIVER & BOYD

EDINBURGH
LONDON

OLIVER AND BOYD LTD
Tweeddale Court
Edinburgh 1

39A Welbeck Street
London W1

First published 1968

Printed in Great Britain by
T. and A. Constable Ltd.
Edinburgh

PREFACE

Not all the essays about European expansion which have
been published since 1951 have stood the test of time as
well as those included in this volume. They are in general
reprinted as they first appeared in *History Today*, though
in some cases with a few minor corrections and revisions.
I am grateful to the respective authors, and to the editors
of *History Today*, for their willing co-operation at all
stages. I would like to thank my colleague Rosemary
Tyzack for helpful advice on the selection, and on the
draft of my introductory essay; also Sara and Alastair
Hargreaves for various forms of assistance in preparing
the volume for publication.

JOHN D. HARGREAVES

CONTENTS

John D. Hargreaves

EUROPEAN EXPANSION AND ITS HISTORIANS

It is almost a truism that what historians write about the past is greatly influenced by what they think about the present. Periods of change and controversy may thus be fruitful in historical re-appraisals. The years since the first publication of *History Today* have seen many revolutionary changes, but few more profound than those in relations between Europe and the former colonial world. In January 1951 it was still not clear that the impact of the Second World War on the overseas empires of the belligerents would prove fatal. Although already the withdrawal of Dutch, American, and British power from Indonesia, the Philippines, and the Indian sub-continent was virtually complete, Frenchmen were fighting to retain the states of Indo-China within the still inchoate French Union, British troops held Malaya against Communist irregular forces, and Soviet Russia still occupied Port Arthur and Dairen. In Africa, with Kwame Nkrumah in Accra prison, hardly anybody dreamed that Ethiopia, Liberia, and Farouk's Egypt represented the nucleus of a continent-wide association of militantly independent states. As late as June 1956 the editors of *History Today* still regarded "the problems of colonial empire" as a theme of pressing contemporary concern. But in the following years they were frequently to find themselves introducing their readers to new nations; countries chiefly known in Britain as colourful "colonial" pages in a stamp album were discovered to have historical personalities of their own. Historical studies, in this journal as elsewhere, were gradually becoming less parochial or Eurocentric; activities of Europeans were recognised as merely one sector of the record of human experience which historians seek to interpret to their contemporaries. Africa, Asia, and Latin America now enjoy positions in European University syllabuses, and in the historical community generally, which would have been hard to envisage in 1951.

Some historians believe that these winds of change have blown their colleagues too far from their traditional routes. Their objections, though sometimes intemperately stated, are partly based on a valid perception of the special roles which peoples of European descent have played in world history during the last four or five centuries. Even though Chinese science, Arab scholarship, Persian painting, African sculpture, Indian craftsmanship, may at one time or another have surpassed the achievements of European contemporaries; in the modern world it has been ideas and institutions of European or North Atlantic origin which, supported by superior economic resources and technological versatility, have exercised the greatest influence—have, indeed, largely defined the very concept of modernity. The political empires founded by Europeans may now seem more or less transitory phenomena—effective in Goa for four and a half centuries, but in Ethiopia for hardly as many years. They may however also appear as merely one phase in a much more enduring process—an expansion of Europe which has not been merely political and military, but social, economic, and cultural too.

Expansion in this sense was a continuing and complex process. The attempts of the textbooks to distinguish phases of "imperialism" and "anti-imperialism" in the policies of European states (which when scrutinised usually prove unsatisfactory and full of contradictions) have only secondary importance, as reflexions of temporary shifts of interest, or of political reactions to colonial disasters. There seems to be a broader interest and significance in relating the changing manifestations of Europeans' activity on the distant frontiers of their influence to profound developments within their own society. Already in later medieval Europe the strength of Crusading movements showed that ambitious individuals and social groups were seeking wider fields of activity overseas; in accordance with the values of the period they naturally and without hypocrisy expressed their aspirations in the form of plans to strengthen and expand the power of Christendom. Hence the legend of Prester John, born, as Dr Lamb shows,[1] at a critical time for the Crusading movement, would have "a profound effect on the history of European exploration and discovery in Asia and Africa" over many centuries.

Nevertheless, this effect could not be fully felt until

[1] See "Prester John", pp. 22-38.

developments in techniques of navigation and warfare had enlarged the possibilities of European expansion. The Portugese chronicler Azurara, in a well-known analysis of the motives of Prince Henry the Navigator in promoting the fifteenth-century voyages of discovery, mentions his desire "to know if there were in those parts any Christian princes, in whom the charity and the love of Christ was so ingrained that they would aid him against those enemies of the faith", and to obtain "knowledge . . . of the land of Prester John". But on Azurara's own showing other motives than pure crusading zeal inspired the Portugese thrust down the African coast; by mid-century, he regretfully noted, after reckoning up the number of souls already saved, "the affairs of these parts were henceforth treated more by trafficking and bargaining of merchants than by bravery and toil in arms".[2] In the Indian Ocean, where the prizes were greater, Vasco da Gama and the men who followed him began to enforce their will on Asian and African rulers by threats and fire-power. St Francis Xavier noted in 1545 "a power, which I may call irresistible, to thrust men headlong into the abyss, where besides the seductions of gain, and the easy opportunities of plunder, their appetites for gain will be sharpened for having tasted it, and there will be a whole torrent of low examples and evil customs to sweep them away".[3] Thus an expansionist movement which initially had something in common with the last

[2] Gomes Eannes de Azurara, *The Chronicle of the Discovery and Conquest of Guinea*, ed. C. R. Beazley and E. Prestage. London (Hakluyt Society) 1896, 1899. I., pp. 28, 55; II., pp. 288-9.

[3] Quoted in Basil Davidson, *Old Africa Rediscovered*, London (Gollancz) 1959, p. 168.

wave of the Crusades now seemed to foreshadow imperialistic drives for power and profit.

The change was of course not merely a matter of moral degeneracy and corruption among the individuals who pioneered the expansion of Europe in the service of Portugal and Spain. Economic and social change in Europe—the development of merchant capitalism, for short—was producing new groups of men for whom the mainspring of action was quite openly and explicitly the desire to expand trade and amass wealth—not merely, like the pioneers of Spanish enterprise in the Americas, by extracting treasure and precious metals but by establishing regular business relations with non-European peoples. It was not in the Iberian peninsula that such men were most numerous or most influential. In the Dutch Republic the "love of gain" (and the necessity of seeking it beyond the restricted territories liberated from Spanish rule) led in the seventeenth century to a remarkable development of maritime enterprise, backed by the growing commercial and financial expertise of great merchant companies chartered by the state—the characteristic engine of European expansion in the seventeenth century. Professor Boxer, in his study of Cornelis Speelman,[4] shows how their trading activities led in time to the establishment of formal overseas dependencies, including the vast and populous Indonesian empire. But political power was rarely sought for its own sake. What these companies initially wanted was to exclude European rivals or interlopers from the countries where they hoped

[4] See "Ledger and Sword: Cornelis Speelman and the Growth of Dutch Power in Indonesia, 1666-1684", pp. 39-54.

to find their profits, and to induce the local rulers to provide the facilities and conditions judged necessary for "peaceful trade". As Sir Keith Hancock wrote in a different context "commerce cannot flourish unless it is given the shelter of a *pax*". So long as local governments were strong and stable enough to administer laws which the traders could accept, few problems arose. Where they were weak (or were weakened by the activities of the foreigners), or represented values and interests antagonistic to those of the Europeans, a satisfactory *pax* was harder to establish. Many agents of European influence found, like Speelman in Java and the Celebes, that it was expedient to challenge the conditions imposed upon their commercial activities, to intervene in civil wars and disputed successions, to deal forcibly with patriotic or religious resistance movements provoked by their own activities. In Indonesia, as in British India, the creation of a formal, unified, colonial empire was a gradual process; it needs to be understood not as a planned but vacillating colonial policy, but as part of this still longer and more complex process of the expansion of Europe's commercial and cultural frontiers.

During the seventeenth and eighteenth centuries, as such activities were intensified in countries accessible from the coastlines of Asia, Africa, and the Americas, economic growth in Europe accelerated, culminating in the organisational and technological innovations associated with the British Industrial Revolution. Exactly how much of this growth was based upon the re-investment of profits derived from the Eastern or Atlantic trades—or, to put the point more bluntly, how far the coming leap in the wealth of the North Atlantic world was based on exploitation of non-European peoples—has not been accurately measured. What is clear is that as Europeans grew richer the rest of the world became—perhaps not absolutely poorer, but more dependent economically and politically on decisions taken in European cities. The extension of the political power of the British East India Company provided the Directors, and the Ministers who increasingly supervised their actions, with the means of controlling the once-flourishing indigenous economy; African slaves, shipped across the Atlantic in increasing numbers by all the maritime powers, were harnessed to the commercialised economy of West Indian sugar islands, and later of cotton plantations in the southern United States; settlers in North America struggled to control the fur trade—and at the same time encroached increasingly on Indian territory. In the eighteenth century empire seemed to orthodox statesmen the way to wealth; not only Spaniards and Dutchmen but now especially the French and the British increasingly fought their wars in and for Canada, India, the West Indian islands. Britain's loss of the American colonies, and the revolution in economic thought associated with Adam Smith, modified the emphasis of the conventional wisdom; "trade, not dominion" became something of a watchword. Yet where dominion was excercised, there was little sign that it would be given up, and trade proved a more powerful motor than formerly for extending the frontiers of European influence.

That influence began to spread further afield. Eighteenth-century men of science and reason—who might also be men of business—became increasingly interested in extending their scientific and geographical knowledge of the world. Sir Joseph Banks—President of the Royal Society, companion of Cook and patron of Flinders and Bligh, founder member of the Association for promoting Discovery of the Inland Parts of Africa, and sponsor of the study of natural history throughout the world— illustrates the enthusiam and range of interests which characterised this generation. La Pérouse's ill-fated ex-pedition to the Pacific in 1785, sponsored by the French monarchy as part of a renewed drive to expand its in-fluence in various parts of the world, was accompanied by an astronomer, a hydrographer, a mineralogist, and several students of natural history: it was equipped with chemical laboratories and a library of 1000 volumes. The versatility of its company was surpassed only by the great team of *savants* who accompanied Napoleon's Egyptian expedition of 1798.

Close behind the explorers, if not actually in their com-pany, came new waves of European expansion, vari-ously represented by traders and whalers, missionaries and mining prospectors, rogues and remittance men. Peter Dillon, whose varied and colourful career in the South Seas is outlined by Professor Davidson,[5] may serve as a representative figure. During the long peace of the nine-teenth century, the developing countries of Europe and North America sent out to the rapidly advancing frontiers of their world a whole range of more or less dynamic and forceful characters—captains of commerce, savers of souls, and often simple misfits. MacGregor Laird and

[5] See "Peter Dillon and the South Seas, pp. 55-76.

Stamford Raffles, David Livingstone and Davy Crockett, testified in their various ways to the new release of energy in the Atlantic world, which the Industrial Revolution signalled. Equipped with their samples or their prayer-books, precision firearms or cheap liquor, such men became diversely involved in the affairs of every community of men in the world, whether or not it had already passed under some colonial flag; old, proud civilisations like China, Japan, Persia, and Turkey, new Republics like those of Latin America, simple societies in Africa and Oceania, all found that in some way or other they had to come to terms with expanding Europe. If they could not provide the *pax* which the newcomers demanded, European warships or consuls were liable to appear to compel them to do so.

Growing appreciation of the rich complexity of these processes underlies the shifting emphasis of historical studies. Studies of governmental policies overseas remain indisputably important (besides being relatively easy to document satisfactorily), but many historians now find greater interest in studying the social environment out of which different groups of Europeans were moved to cross the seas, and the way in which these people reacted to and were changed by their new conditions of life. Such an approach has of course long been practised in countries such as Canada and Australia—not to mention the U.S.A.—formed by the settlement of substantial populations of European origin. In Britain studies of what were formerly called the "white dominions" long formed the core of surveys of imperial history. More recently, as the emphasis of this volume shows, the effect of

E.E.—B

decolonisation and the mounting claims for recognition by the under-privileged peoples of the world has been to attract attention to the responses made by non-Europeans to the growing demands of Europe and to the development of their position with colonial society.

Nowhere is this problem more acute and intricate, historically or actually, than in South Africa. What South African writers and statesmen at one time described as "the race problem" was really a political and cultural problem—that of the relationship within South Africa of communities of Afrikaner and British origin, and of the various interests they represented. The antithesis between representatives of "the non-industrial and non-literary habits of the eighteenth century" and of thrusting nineteenth-century capitalism (with its penumbra of sometimes rather watery philanthrophy) was more stark and striking in South Africa than almost anywhere in Europe. But, from the 1930s, South African writers like C. W. de Kiewiet and J. S. Marais—and soon afterwards the Australian Hancock—began to show greater interest in the role of Africans and other non-European groups within South African society; even if the political and legislative history of the Union might seem to be pointing towards the apartheid system formalised after 1948, its social and economic history was a record of interaction and increasing mutual dependence. This underlying interdependence of the diverse and antagonistic communities is well brought out in Mr and Mrs Bradlow's retelling of the story of the population movements which have produced the modern Republic of South Africa.[6] It is fair to

[6] See "Trek and Counter-trek in South Africa", pp. 77-92.

add that for them as for most other writers the framework is still set by the conventional colonial record, and that much remains to be discovered about the life of African communities within modern South African society. For insight into this great subject it is perhaps still best to turn to a pioneer work which, when first published in 1945, seemed wildly eccentric to the mainstream of South African historiography—Bishop Bengt Sundkler's *Bantu Prophets in South Africa*. If industrial growth and the spread of Christianity were among the consequences of the expansion of European frontiers in southern Africa, so too were social deprivation, and desperate sectarian attempts to find some hope of a juster order, either in this world or the next.

In most of the rest of Africa, the re-orientation of historiography was slower to begin, though in recent years it has moved very much more rapidly. Writers on colonial history commonly assumed that European expansion in tropical Africa was a record of how peoples of superior culture, whether impelled by missionary duty or by "love of gain", gradually imposed superior forms of life upon uncomprehending and ungrateful illiterates. The first, and for long the standard, historian of the partition of Africa, J. S. Keltie, regarded his theme as the record of how "the bulk of the one barbarous continent [was] parcelled out amongst the most civilized powers of Europe". Research and reflexion by historians from many continents, especially since the impetus to decolonisation provided by the Second World War, have shown that the sources for studying genuinely African history (before as well as during the period of European impact) are much more extensive and rewarding than was commonly assumed. They provide evidence of African statecraft and social adaptability which puts the European partition in a very different light; it seems more like the culmination (in some ways, certainly, sudden and unexpected) of a period of Afro-European relations which had already significantly affected the history of both continents.

The effects of such new perspectives on popularly accepted views can be neatly illustrated by the way in which British relations with the Nilotic Sudan in the later nineteenth century have been presented to the general public. As Professor Holt points out, British writing on the subject long concentrated on two more or less romantic heroes, Gordon and Kitchener, faced with what G. M. Trevelyan called "the barbarism of the Sudanese tribes".[7] Even those who respected the bravery of "Fuzzy-Wuzzy" rarely went beyond Kipling's famous tribute—"a pore benighted heathen, but a first-class fighting man". Yet a recent film spectacular featured the leading British actor, carefully schooled in the pronunciation of Arabic, in a dignified portrayal of the Mahdi, Muhammad Ahmad. Such shifts in sympathy and emphasis may be indirectly influenced by the work of historians like Professor Holt. His article on the Madhia, and his book on the same subject, illustrate both the importance of studying the effects of the expansion of Europe from the "receiving end", and the rich possibilities for doing so which may

[7] See "The Mahdia in the Sudan, 1881-1898", pp. 93-111. Norman Daniel in *Islam, Europe and Empire*, Edinburgh (University Press) 1966, has recently shown how in early writing about the Mahdia (largely inspired by Wingate) attitudes characteristic of modern imperialism merged with anti-Muslim prejudices of earlier centuries.

be seized by historians equipped to use unconventional evidence. It is true that historians elsewhere in Africa may not be so fortunate as Professor Holt, who as Government Archivist in the Sudan was able to use the Arabic-language archives of the Mahdist state—though elsewhere in Islamic Africa too it is now clear that comparable archival materials have survived the neglect of the colonial period. Even where African rulers did not use written documents, it may prove extremely rewarding to turn to the oral traditions of the state authority, or to evidence recorded by literate outsiders—colonial officials, missionaries, Western-educated Africans—who may not always have appreciated its full significance.

The Mahdist state represents an attempt at self-renewal by a Muslim society challenged by the growing influence of Europe—in this case mediated through its Egyptian overlords. It represents a positive response to the challenge of modernisation, which was destroyed because it happened to lie at the cross-roads of rival European imperialisms. It has not so far in this essay been necessary to use this emotive term, which Europeans themselves did not apply to colonial expansion before the 1870s. Its use was developed, as the late Professor Koebner showed, by British critics of Disraeli's later policies: but it entered into wide and general currency with the sudden scramble of European states for territory in Africa and the Pacific in the 1880s and 1890s, and the simultaneous intensification of their struggle for advantages (not always implying territorial sovereignty) in the independent states of Asia. These new developments had profound effects not merely on the territories brought under foreign rule, but on the internal life of the European states, and their relations with one another; this struggle for the division of the non-European world seemed liable to lead to international war among European powers. These drastic reversals of policies followed by Governments in the earlier nineteenth century set contemporaries searching for explanations, and launched the great debate, which still continues, about the origins of this "new imperialism".

This essay is hardly the place to attempt to sum up a discussion in which much intellectual and emotional capital has been invested by many wise men. A few observations, however, are relevant. Firstly, the new imperialism seems much less revolutionary when viewed in the context of the "expansion of Europe" than if government policies alone are considered. The reluctance to acquire formal colonies which affected European—especially British—statesmen during the earlier nineteenth century in no way impeded the continuing flow of "frontiersmen" into other continents. Sometimes the activities of these men had created interests which their governments were led—with more or less reluctance—to protect by the erection or extension of a colonial government; almost everywhere their presence created some sort of local reaction with which they would sooner or later have expected their governments to deal. There was nothing new about a French government interesting itself in Dahomey, or about British or German activity in Samoa; the novelty lay in governmental policies directed to the establishment of formal sovereignty. And for such changes explanations may reasonably be sought in

European politics, as well as in the changing nature of the European interests involved.

Secondly, while the expansion of Europe took many forms, sending out the disinterested as well as the avaricious, saints and scholars as well as ruffians and rogues, it seems pointless to deny that its mainspring was the dynamism of the developing economies of Europe. Contemporary participants would have been astonished that anybody should deny that in *this* sense expansion had economic roots. The debate about the new imperialism which Hobson and Lenin inaugurated rests however on more specific assertions: that the dominant role in European capitalism was passing to powerful banks and finance houses; that (failing such a great expansion in European markets as might be achieved by enlarging the purchasing-power of the working-class) they could only maintain the rate of profit on invested capital by obtaining dependable and exclusive outlets overseas; that the struggle of rich capitalist monopolies to control such outlets was leading to the territorial partition of the world. These are hypotheses about European economic history which it is not easy to substantiate (or to refute) by scrutinising specific examples of overseas expansion; historians who concentrate on particular areas may be more impressed by the complexity of the local situation, and the roles played by individual personalities, than by any evident manifestations of such generalised and imperial forces.

Of course, there were many cases where financial manipulators and monopolists were superseding traders as the driving force of the European frontier; Dr Blakemore's lively study of J. T. North's activities in Chile provides an excellent and little-known example.[8] Yet the startling increase in British investment during the 1880s did not result in any extension of formal imperialist control; Americans might dub Chile "nothing more than an English colony", but, even if all the charges brought against North of improper intervention in its affairs are accepted, it in fact remained a great deal less, as any Asian or African subject of the new empires could have testified.

More promising examples of finance capital preparing the way for formal colonial expansion might seem to be provided by the activities of Leopold II of Belgium and his association in the Congo, and by the remarkable financial and political empire of Cecil Rhodes in South Africa; the latter case particularly had a profound influence on the formulation of the theory of capitalist imperialism. Yet on closer inspection there are difficulties even here in fitting the evidence to the theory. Leopold originally envisaged imperialism as a national policy, which besides bringing economic benefits to Belgians would divert their attention from parochial sectarianism and class-conflict. When the politicians proved uninterested he created a personal empire which literally exploited the Congo basin by rapaciously depleting its resources of ivory and rubber for the sake of quick returns. But this was not to provide outlets for surplus Belgian capital, for initially capitalists fought shy of Africa, and Leopold had to finance his schemes by manipulating public funds; and though later the financiers moved in, for Leopold the profits of the Congo became a means of strengthening the constitutional position of the Belgian

[8] See "John Thomas North, the Nitrate King", pp. 111-30.

monarchy, and erecting grandiose public works to com-
memorate his own reign. Nor is it really satisfactory to
type-cast Rhodes as a characteristic finance capitalist;
that role might be better filled by other Rand potentates
such as J. B. Robinson, whose aim was not to conquer
the Transvaal but "to make money in peace".[9] Far from
seeking an empire to protect his investments, Rhodes
seemed to have planned his investments with the aim of
creating his own sort of empire. In explaining the influence
of men like these in the partition of Africa it is necessary
to take account of their political designs and ambitions as
well as of the economic interests of their class.

There are other cases where political designs very
clearly predominate. German traders and missionaries
had become increasingly active in Africa and the South
Seas during the nineteenth century; yet it is generally
accepted that Bismarck's decisions to establish formal
colonies in 1884-5 were primarily determined by calculations of international and internal political advantage.
Italian politicians sought to distract attention from the
unsolved problems of the new monarchy by successes
abroad—turning to Africa when the weakness of their
international position precluded further territorial gains
in the Adriatic. Military men played a greater role than
capitalists in the overland expansion of Russia's Asian
empire, a process which so much preoccupied the British
men of India, during the nineteenth century: the slowly
developing Russian economy needed to import rather
than to export capital. In West Africa much of France's

[9] J. S. Marais, *The Fall of Kruger's Republic*, Oxford (Clarendon)
1961, p. 139.

new empire was conquered by military officers, anxious to atone for the defeat of 1870 and thereby win glory and promotion in the service for themselves. In their semi-autonomous command of French Sudan they were able to launch and pursue campaigns without effective control from more cautious superiors in Paris, and with open contempt for the much less bellicose conceptions of Empire held by French merchants.

Multiplication of such examples is unlikely to clinch the argument about the new imperialism, but may show that any monolithic theory will fail to do full justice to the various forms in which the expansion of Europe now approached its climax. Europeans continued to go to distant places with many varied motives, and for all sorts of purposes; and not all of them desired or welcomed the intervention of a government to establish a formal colonial administration. Nevertheless, this wave of de-liberate political empire-building was a logical culmi-nation of earlier European expansion. To control their new dependencies the European powers devised insti-tutions and methods which not merely safeguarded most of the economic interests of their subjects but gave expression to the political and moralistic purposes of late nineteenth-century imperialists. For among the most novel characteristics of this period was the emergence of administrators and politicians who saw in the exercise of beneficent paternal rule over other peoples a respon-sibility for which the labours of earlier generations pro-vided merely a preparation.

Mr Edwardes's account of how Curzon conceived and discharged that responsibility thus forms an appropriate conclusion to this volume.[10] While illustrating the confidence of the great pro-consuls in the power of efficient and scientifically enlightened administration to induce improvement, both material and moral, in the condition of their subjects, it also suggests how even the most powerful of imperial governments tended to overestimate their capacity to control the course of change. Few colonial governments had more than modest success in promoting economic growth for the general benefit of their subjects; and those that succeeded best thereby initiated social ferments which would undermine the fabric of imperial rule. The very unity which the British prided themselves on bringing to India (like the Dutch in Indonesia, the French in *Afrique Occidentale*) provided the framework for new varieties of anti-colonial nationalism. As in all the best families, even the most benevolent paternalism tended to produce rebellion in the younger generation. Economic development, however stunted, produced groups of men ill at ease in the colonial framework, whose leaders found within the imperial myth itself weapons for attacking the basic assumptions of alien rule. And, because some Europeans took the moralistic myths seriously, they could also find allies within the imperial powers; the expansion of Europe involved even the expansion of European liberalism, as was shown by the role of the retired civil servant A. O. Hume (son of the British radical Joseph Hume) in founding the Indian National Congress. Curzon may have seen the true spirit of India in the cultural monuments of past civilisations which he worked to preserve: but a more notable

[10] See "The Viceroyalty of Lord Curzon", pp. 131-53.

feature of his time in India was the development of the politically orientated culture represented by those angry young Congress leaders whom he despised.

During the twentieth century these self-liquidating forces within the colonial empires were reinforced by the impact of international war and revolution. The overseas power of European states proved more ephemeral than could have been credited by those who shared the euphoric self-confidence which characterised Queen Victoria's Jubilee of 1897. But, just as political imperialism was only one aspect of European expansion, its liquidation does not mark the end of European influence. Independent nations, aspiring to improve the condition of their peoples in a world whose economic systems seem weighted against them, are well aware that foreign influence may still be exercised by indirect methods; this is what they mean by "neo-colonialism". Yet they do not reject machines and techniques, scientific knowledge, even forms of ecomonic organisation which have been developed in Europe and North America, but accept them (sometimes, indeed, uncritically) as legitimate tools for improving their own condition. More than this: leaders seeking to define an autochthonous political culture still draw, though selectively, on European intellectual traditions—on Marx and Mill, Lenin and Napoleon, Adam Smith and Keynes. Intellectually the expansion of Europe is not over, although it may now be more fruitfully regarded as part of a reciprocal process to which Asian and African contributions are also important.

One of the liberating effects of political decolonisation has been to permit a growth of uninhibited dialogue between former "rulers" and "subject peoples". As already suggest, historians have been among the first to benefit from this. There is little doubt that *History Today* will, during its second fifreen years, contain an increasing number of discussions of European expansion from African or Asian viewpoints; and that these will not merely draw attention to portions of the record previously forgotten or distorted but will provide penetrating critiques of the development of European society itself. If the language of these continues to be as mild and generous as has often been the case so far, historians at least will know better than to treat this as a reason for national complacency.

Alastair Lamb

PRESTER JOHN[1]

The history of Prester John is the history of a man who
never existed. Medieval legend called him into being when
it was felt that his presence would be of help in the
struggle between Christian Europe and the Islamic world.
His name was first recorded in 1145 and continued to
appear from time to time up to the beginning of the seventeenth century. Each reference to Prester John—John the
Priest—was compounded of two elements; on one side
the European wish for the existence of a strong Christian
power beyond the confines of Medieval Christendom; on
the other, some historical event or process in a far corner
of the earth, on the distorted news of which was based a
concrete shape for this wish. Originally the Priest King
was heard of in Asia; later it became generally accepted
that his kingdom lay in Africa. With the growth of
geographical knowledge and the discovery of places in
which Prester John was not to be found, so was the
location of the Priest King moved to lesser-known regions.
The development of the legend makes a fascinating study;

[1] [Copyright © Alastair Lamb. Originally published in *History
Today*, VII (1957), pp. 313-21.]

not only for the sake of its wealth of fabulous detail but also because the belief in the existence of Prester John had a profound effect on the history of European exploration and discovery in Asia and Africa.

Many elements in the corpus of medieval mythology played their part in paving the way for the appearance of the Priest King. The legends of the exploits in Asia of Alexander the Great contained many details of the wonders which could be expected in the Orient. The associated story of Gog and Magog and of the wall which Alexander built to prevent these malevolent people from devastating the civilised world gave strength to the idea that the safety of Christendom might depend upon some force without its borders. The story of the Magi, the three wise Kings of the East who brought gifts to the infant Jesus, suggested that there might be as yet undiscovered Eastern rulers who were true friends to the Christian faith. The Jewish belief in the existence of the Lost Ten Tribes of Israel in some part of furthest Asia, perhaps beyond the wall of Gog and Magog, strengthened this concept of salvation from without by its implication that the long-awaited Jewish Messiah might arise from among these excluded tribes. Finally, there was the fact of the early spread of Christianity to remote corners of Asia which had given rise to legends concerning the missions of the Apostle St Thomas to India and China.

The Christian communities of the Far East, though generally schismatic or heretical, never lost touch with the Christians of Europe. The Holy Land provided a meeting place for Christians from all over the world. On occasions representatives of remote churches found their way to Rome. It is probable that such a visit, that of the Patriarch John of the Indian Church of St Thomas to Rome in about 1122, might have provided the immediate basis of the legend of Prester John, the Christian Priest King in the East.

Patriarch John did his best to impress his Roman brothers in Christ. He told such fabulous tales that Pope Calixtus II is said to have asked him to keep silent, and only permitted him to continue his account when the good Patriarch took an oath on the Gospels that all he said was true. He told of his wonderful capital, Ulna, so vast in area that it took four days to walk round its walls. He described the Phison, one of the rivers of Paradise, which watered his land. He gave an account of the miraculous body of St Thomas which lay preserved at Ulna and was the chief glory of his see. He gave the impression that he was the temporal as well as the spiritual ruler of this Indian state. He might well have suggested that he could be a most valuable ally to Christendom in time of need.

In 1145, when the Prester first appears, need for such an ally was all too apparent. The capture of Edessa by the Seljuk general Zengi in 1144 marked the turning-point in the history of the Crusades. The conquests of the First Crusade were gravely endangered by a revival of Islamic power. The news of the fall of Edessa was brought to Pope Eugenius III from the Levant by Hugh, Bishop of Jabala in Syria. The meeting between Bishop and Pope, at Viterbo in the autumn of 1145, was attended by the German chronicler Otto of Freisingen, who took down what was said.

To the Bishop the gloomy news of the fall of Edessa

was balanced by the prospect of help for the Crusaders from an unsuspected direction. The Bishop had heard that not long ago "one John, king and priest, who dwells in the extreme Orient beyond Persia and Armenia, and is with his people a Christian, but a Nestorian", had defeated the Persians and captured their capital. After this victory John set out with his army to come to the aid of the Crusaders, but was unable to get his troops across the Tigris. He marched north up the river in hopes of finding a place where the water froze over in winter. In this he was disappointed, and after waiting some time for a frost which never came, and losing many of his men owing to the unfavourable climate, he was obliged to turn homewards. This Prester John, the Bishop concluded,

> was said to be of the ancient race of those Magi who were mentioned in the Gospel, and to rule the same nations as they did, and to have such glory and wealth that he used only an emerald sceptre. It was from his being fired by the example of his fathers, who came to adore Christ in his cradle, that he was proposing to go to Jerusalem when he was prevented by the cause already alleged.

There is a certain basis of contemporary fact behind this odd story. In 1141 the Seljuk Sultan Sinjar, in one of the decisive battles in the history of Central Asia, was defeated at Katwan near Samarcand by a Mongol people, the Kara Kitai, who had recently migrated to Central Asia from their previous home in North China. The Kara, or "black", Kitai were a branch of the Kitans who had ruled over North China from 936 until 1122, when they had been dispossessed by another Mongolian group, the Kin. One branch remained under Kin domination; another branch set out on a migration which, in a few years, brought it to the borders of the Seljuk empire. It is from the name of these people, the Kitai, that the name which Marco Polo gave to China, Cathay, is derived. Their defeat of Sinjar marked the end of Seljuk expansion and, in the Levant, paved the way for the rise of Saladin. To the Crusaders of the time, however, it must have seemed as if some unknown ally was fighting on their side against their chief enemy, the Seljuks.

The Prester John of this story is the Emperor of the Kara Kitai, the Gurkhan, Yeliu Tashi by name. Yeliu Tashi was certainly no Christian; if anything, he was Buddhist. Attempts have been made to derive the name John from the title Gurkhan: but there is no need for this. To the Bishop it sufficed that the victor over the Seljuks was no Moslem. The name John probably came from a memory of the visit of the Patriarch John of India to Rome in 1122.

The victories of Prester John failed to relieve the position of the Crusaders. His armies did not appear. Without him the Second Crusade ended miserably. But the Priest King's failure to bring succour to his co-religionists did not weaken their faith in his existence. Any lingering doubts, moreover, must have been dispelled in 1165, when the Byzantine Emperor Manuel Comnenos, the Emperor Frederick Barbarossa, and the Pope all received a letter from the fabulous Prester John. The letter was a forgery. It may have been intended as a tract on the benefits of priestly government and hence as a useful support to the Papacy in relation to the Empire.

It may have been devised as propaganda for a Third Crusade. It enjoyed a very wide circulation, and its popularity was such that it continued to be copied, with frequent topical interpolations, throughout the rest of the Middle Ages. More than one hundred manuscript copies of the letter, in several languages, are known to exist.

The bulk of the letter was devoted to describing the magnificence of the Kingdom of Prester John, with a wealth of detail derived from such diverse sources as the various Alexander legends, and the story of the city of the Apostle Thomas which Patriarch John told the Pope in 1122. The location of the Prester's kingdom is in India. He worshipped at the Church of St Thomas. He informed the leaders of Europe that

> We have determined to visit the sepulchre of our Lord with a very large army, in accordance with the glory of our majesty, to humble and chastise the enemies of the cross of Christ and to exalt His blessed name.

In 1177 the Pope Alexander III replied with a long letter to Prester John. The immediate occasion for this was a meeting by the Pope's doctor, one Philip, with some representative of the Priest King while on pilgrimage to the Holy Land. According to Philip, Prester John, a Nestorian, wished to embrace the Roman faith and to build a church in Rome and an altar in the Church of the Holy Sepulchre at Jerusalem. When the Pope heard this, he promptly sent Philip as bearer of a friendly letter to the Prester. Where Philip went, and what became of the letter, is not recorded. It is possible that Philip had met in Jerusalem pilgrims from one of the remoter Christian communities of Central Asia and interpreted what they told him in the light of his preconceptions about Prester John. Doubtless, the Pope, who had just emerged victorious from a long struggle with Frederick Barbarossa, saw no harm in letting it be known that he had established relations with this fabulous Christian power of the East. The episode certainly received much publicity; various versions of the Pope's letter are given in several English chronicles of the thirteenth century.

When news of Prester John next emerged from the East, in about 1221, the need for outside assistance for the Crusaders was even greater than it had been in 1145. In 1187 Jerusalem fell to Saladin. The Third Crusade, in which Richard Coeur de Lion won such fame, failed to recapture the Holy City. The Fourth Crusade, instead of bringing help to Palestine, sacked the Christian city of Constantinople and seriously weakened the remaining vigour of the Byzantine Empire. The Children's Crusade of 1212 ended in tragedy. The army of the Fifth Crusade, which landed in Egypt in 1218, sorely needed some *deus ex machina* to bring to it greater success than that met with by its predecessors.

Hope for such help was suggested in the letter which Jacques de Vitry, Bishop of Ptolemais, wrote to Pope Honorius III in 1221. He reported that David, King of India and descendant of Prester John, had attacked the infidel with three armies, and that one of these armies was at that moment within fifteen days' march of Antioch. Here at last, he wrote, was the long-awaited "Hammer of the Infidel". This news was also welcomed by the Jewish peoples of the Levant, who saw in David their Messiah, perhaps because of some confusion between "Rex Indorum" and "Rex Judeorum".

There is little difficulty in detecting the Central Asian origin of this story. In 1218 the Mongols, under Genghis Khan, overthrew the Kara Kitai Empire which had in about 1211 passed under the control of an adventurer of the Naiman tribe of Mongols, Kutchluk by name. By 1220 Ghenghis Khan had gone on to destroy the Empire of Kwarezm, a powerful Islamic state which had been founded towards the end of the twelfth century in the land between the Rivers Oxus and Jaxartes, and which extended its influence over much of Persia. In 1221 a flying column of Mongol troops dashed into Persia, nearly captured Baghdad, and penetrated far into the Caucasus. David, of the line of Prester John, could only be Genghis Khan.

Today, the picture of Genghis Khan in the role of saviour of Christendom seems absurd. In the early thirteenth century it seemed reasonable enough. It was well known that several nomadic tribes in Central Asia had embraced Christianity. Even if the Mongol Khans were not of the faith, this was no reason why they should not be converted into genuine Prester Johns. Pope Innocent IV, who was elected in 1243, certainly thought along these lines. He had been told that "the Mongols worship one God, and were not without some religious beliefs". The Mongols, moreover, "say they have Saint John the Baptist for Chief". So reported a Russian Bishop who had fled to France to escape the advancing Mongol hordes. Innocent resolved to try to establish some sort of relations with the Mongols.

In 1245 Friar John of Plano Carpini was sent by the Pope to carry letters to the Mongol Khan, and there can be little doubt that among his instructions was a request to clear up the mystery of Prester John. His conclusion was that the Mongols were not the people of the Priest King: but his information about who was Prester John is not so definite and varies according to different versions of the narrative which he wrote on his return from his mission. Carpini had a passing reference to the Black Cathayans, who, he claimed, were Christian in all but name. They had recently been conquered by the Mongols. But the Prester was not among these people who had given rise to the story of 1145; he had moved to the adjacent land of India Major, if one is permitted to inter-pret "the black Saracens who are also called Ethiopians" as a reference to the Black, or Kara, Kitai. In the thirteenth century, it is worth noting, the term Ethiopia was so im-precise as not to justify its location in Africa without sup-porting evidence which, in this case, is not present.

Prester John, Carpini wrote, lived beside these "black Saracens". Genghis Khan tried to invade his land but was repelled by the Prester, who sent against the invading troops what sounds very much like explosive charges fastened to the backs of horses and set off at the right moment by suicide soldiers. But another version of Carpini told a different story. Prester John and his son David were described as kings of India to whom the Mongols used to pay tribute. Genghis Khan, however, put an end to this practice by invading the land of Prester John and defeating King David. The victorious Prester is in the tradition of the stories of 1145 and 1221; the defeated Prester fits in with the travellers' tales of the second half of the thirteenth century.

Just as the Pope was interested in finding Christian allies in the East, so was the Crusading French King, Louis IX. Louis had met Carpini after his return, and had talked with other envoys whom the Pope had sent to various Mongol Khans. In 1253, after his unfortunate Egyptian Crusade, Louis sent his own envoy to the Mongols, Friar William of Rubruck, and once more it is most probable that the ambassador to the Mongols was instructed to keep on the look-out for traces of Prester John. These Rubruck had no difficulty in finding, but they were hardly of the type which Louis would have hoped for.

This was Rubruck's story. In about 1098 there lived in Central Asia a certain Con Khan, chief of the Black Cathayans. When Con died the Black Cathayans came under the rule of a certain Naiman chief, a Nestorian Christian known as John. John had a brother, Unc, who ruled over the Kerait people in the neighbourhood of Karakorum, the Mongol capital. The Keraits were also Nestorians, but Unc abandoned the religion of his people and became an idolater. When King John died, Unc combined the rule of the Black Cathayans with that of the Kerait. With this increase in power Unc's ambition became boundless and soon he attacked the neighbouring tribe of the Mongols and defeated it. Aroused by this disaster, the Mongols made Genghis Khan their leader, and under his guidance soon avenged their defeat by overwhelming in battle the forces of Unc and forcing him to take refuge in Cathay, never again to return to Tartary.

As in the other Prester John stories to this date,

Rubruck's story is not without historical foundation. Con Khan is clearly the Gurkhan of the Kara Kitai. In about 1211 this position was usurped by the Naiman adventurer Kutchluk, who is clearly the model for Rubruck's King John, though there is no evidence that Kutchluk or the Naiman were Christians at the time. Unc is as easily identified. He is Toghrul, chief of the Kerait tribe, who had been given the title of *Wang*, or "King", by the Chinese Kin Dynasty. Toghrul had at one time been the patron of the young Genghis, and had later become his enemy. The defeat of Toghrul by Genghis in 1203 marked the virtual completion of Genghis's unification of the tribes of Mongolia. The connexion between Kutchluk and Toghrul was probably derived from the fact that the Naiman tribe had fought on Toghrul's side in his war with Genghis. A further relationship between the Kara Kitai and Toghrul might have been based on a confusion of the title of the Kara Kitai Emperor, Gurkhan, with the name of Toghrul's father, Gur Khan. The Kerait tribe followed Nestorian Christianity.

A close examination of the Kara Kitai, such as Rubruck was in a position to make, showed that neither were they any longer a power worthy of notice nor had they ever been Christians. The Keraits, while their political importance had greatly declined after the defeat of Toghrul, were still the most important Christian tribe in Central Asia. The conversion of the Keraits took place in about 1009 in miraculous circumstances which were widely reported at the time. The King of the Keraits, so the story went, lost his way when out hunting. A blizzard overtook him and he was convinced his hour had come, when a

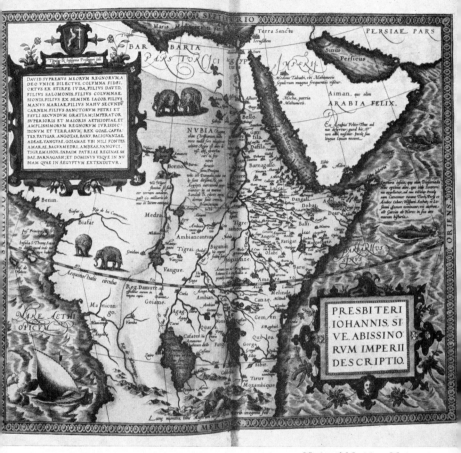

"It was inevitable that the search for Prester John should be shifted to Africa." Map from Ortelius, *Theatrum*, 1573.

"The angry Fijians fought back with vigour and success."
Captain Dillon besieged in Fiji, September, 1813. Col-
oured lithograph by C. Ingrey from the Collection of Rex
D. C. Nan Kivell.

National Library of Australia

D'HEER CORNELIS SPEELMAN: GEBOOREN TOT ROTTERDAM
A°. 1628. RAAT VAN INDIA, OUDT GOUVERNEUR VAN DE CUST COR-
MANDEL, SUPPERINTENDENT ADMIRAEL VELT OVERSTE EN COM-
MISSARIS OVER DE OOSTERSE PROVENTIEN &c.

Den Dapperen Speelman die de trotse Macassaren
Volstreckt verheerde, voor de groote Maetschappy.
Bouten ontsette van haer vyandlycke schaaren,
Molucke vrede voor gedachte dwinglando.
Thoond dus syn wesen, op den throon van syn gelucken.
Syn Staat en Crygscund, u door kunst niet uet te drucken.

Batavia den 10 van Wintermaent 1670.

Cornelis Speelman.

Saint came to him in a vision and said: "If you believe in
Christ, I will lead you in the right direction and you will
not die here". The King got home safely. He remembered
the vision and embraced the Christian faith along with his
tribe, some 200,000 souls. The Keraits were clearly well
suited for the role of the people of Prester John. It is
probable that the story of their conversion played its part
in the development of the legend. Rubruck's narrative
paves the way for the transfer of the title of Prester John
from the Kara Kitai to the Keraits.

By the time Marco Polo set out on his travels the identification of Prester John with the ruler of the Keraits had
become generally accepted. Polo's account of the Prester,
while similar to that of Rubruck, makes no further
mention of the Kara Kitai. Like Rubruck, Marco Polo is
not greatly impressed with the Prester's sanctity. He attri-
butes the defeat of Prester John by Genghis in great part
to the Priest King's pride and lack of tact in dealing with
the Mongols. When Genghis sends ambassadors to John
to seek the Prester's daughter as a wife for the Mongol
ruler, he receives an insulting reply. War follows in which
Prester John is defeated and killed. On the eve of the
battle Christian astrologers prophesy that Genghis will
win, and Genghis is so pleased with this correct prediction
that from that day he always treats Christians "with great
respect" and considers them to be "men of truth for ever
after".

The general trend of the Prester John legend in the
thirteenth century was towards a discrediting of the Priest
King in favour of the Mongols, his conquerors on whose
shoulders, it seemed, had fallen the mantle of the saviours

of Christendom. There was some basis to this concept. Several important Mongol officials were Christian; and several of the clans which had united under the banner of Genghis Khan were of this faith. When, in the years after 1239, it seemed as if the Mongols, who had conquered Russia, Persia, parts of Asia Minor and the Levant, and had penetrated for a brief moment into Poland and Hungary, were destined to play a dominant part in European politics, the idea of a Christian Mongol Empire became most attractive. The value of a Mongol alliance was evident. A Byzantine Emperor did not shrink from giving his daughter in marriage to a Khan of the Mongol Golden Horde in Russia. Frankish princes in the Levant gladly allied themselves to Hulagu. This Mongol satrap, grandson of Genghis Khan, destroyer of the Abbasid Caliphate, and founder of the Il Khan dynasty of Persia, played a part in the Levant in the second half of the thirteenth century not unlike that which it had been hoped at one time Prester John would play. For a while it seemed as if Hulagu would crush the power of Egypt, whose leader, Baibars, was then the mainstay of Islamic power in the Levant. It even seemed possible that Hulagu would become a Christian; his wife was already of that faith.

In these circumstances Prester John dwindled in importance. Marco Polo found a person whom he considered to be descended from Prester John, George by name, who still ruled in the province of Tenduc, in the great loop of the Yellow River, where Polo had located the Priest's realm. George's family married into that of the Great Khan. He still held land, but only as a Mongol feudatory, and he did not hold "anything like the whole of what Prester John once possessed". George was later met by the Franciscan Mission which was established in China under the Mongol peace in the early years of the four-teenth century. One of its members, John of Monte-corvino, converted him to the Catholic faith and per-suaded him to build a Catholic Church at Tenduc. This George, it is now known, was not, in fact, descended from Toghrul, or Wang Khan, but came from the Christian tribe of the Onguts, whose Chinese name of Wang Kou could easily have been confused with that of Wang Khan. Friar Odoric of Pordenone, who travelled widely in Central Asia in the early fourteenth century, formed a poor opinion of this Prester. Information about him was mainly derived from the Nestorians, and Odoric would have been surprised if a hundredth part of what they said were true. The Friar visited Tenduc, the Prester's capital —which he called Tozan—and found it much inferior to the Italian town of Vicenza. It was clear that the Asiatic Prester John had had his day.

By the beginning of the fourteenth century the idea of help for Christendom from the Orient had suffered rude disillusionment. The followers of Hulagu, of whom so much had once been hoped, embraced Islam as did the Mongols in Russia. The centre of Crusading interest, moreover, had been shifting from the Levant to Egypt and North Africa. The pattern had been set by St Louis. It became fixed when Acre, the last Frankish stronghold on the Levant mainland, fell to the Saracens in 1291. The next phase of the Crusade was to be the preparation for Portuguese expansion on to the coast of North Africa.

It was inevitable that the search for Prester John should be shifted to Africa. By the early fourteenth century his kingdom was being located in Abyssinia, where a Christian community had been in existence since the fourth century. Contact between Abyssinia and Europe had been severed by the Islamic conquests of the seventh century: but at the very moment when the Asiatic Prester John was being discredited by travellers like Friar Odoric, Abyssinian embassies began to reach the Courts of Europe and Dominican missionaries were able to penetrate into Central Africa. By the end of the fourteenth century few writers in Europe would have denied that Prester John was the ruler of Abyssinia.

Here, it was argued, he had retired when the Mongols had defeated him in Central Asia. And here he was still able to render valuable assistance to Christendom against the power of Islam in the Mediterranean. In his kingdom lay the source of the River Nile upon which the life of the most formidable Moslem power, Egypt, depended, and he had but to divert the course of this river to starve the Egyptians into submission. That Prester John had not already done so, some writers argued, was solely because the Priest King did not wish to have on his conscience the lives of the many Christians who lived in the Nile Delta. Other observers, less charitably, wrote that the Prester was dissuaded by a large Egyptian subsidy.

In this new role the Priest King was stripped of much of the fabulous and the romantic quality bestowed upon him by the earlier versions of the legend. Even now, however, he had a part to play in the history of exploration, for it was partly in search of his kingdom, in the hope that he would prove an ally in a renewed Crusade, that Prince Henry the Navigator encouraged the series of journeys along the coast of West Africa which were to culminate in the epic voyage of Vasco da Gama and the discovery of the direct sea route to the Indies. Long after Prince Henry's death this search continued, until, in 1493, the Portuguese traveller Covilham, who had been sent out by his king for this purpose, reached Abyssinia and ended, as far as Portugal was concerned, the quest for Prester John. But the Priest King, it now transpired, was neither very wealthy nor very powerful. Far from being a source of strength against Islam, he stood in great need of Portuguese support to save his kingdom from Islamic conquest.

Throughout the fourteenth and fifteenth centuries a few writers and cartographers remained loyal to the Asiatic legend. The discovery that the Abyssinian Prester was but a faint shadow of the great potentate of the earliest versions of the legend may well have suggested that this African king was not, after all, the fabulous Prester John. It is certain that the Jesuit mission which established itself at the Court of the Mogul Emperor Akbar at the end of the sixteenth century thought that the Priest King still ruled in Cathay, that mysterious land described by Marco Polo. It was only after 1603, when a member of that mission, one Benedict Goes, had been despatched to investigate this possibility and in so doing found that Cathay was one and the same as China, a land about which much had been learned during the course of the sixteenth century, that it was concluded that there remained no place on earth where the great Christian king might still reign.

The Portuguese continued to call the Negus of Abyssinia by the name of Prester John, and the rest of the world has followed suit. The name, however, became no more than a convenient title for a minor king. The legend of Prester John, like many other legends of the Middle Ages, fell before the relentless advance of modern geographical knowledge. And yet, in the development of that knowledge, it had played a most significant part. In its youth this legend encouraged the exploration of the land route between Europe and Central Asia and the Far East; in its middle age it assisted the discovery of the direct sea route to the Indies; even at the moment of its death it was still strong enough to lead to the identification of Cathay with the Chinese Empire.

C. R. Boxer

LEDGER AND SWORD

Cornelis Speelman and the Growth
of Dutch Power in Indonesia[1]
1666-1684

When Maria de' Medici, the exiled Queen-Mother of
France, visited the new and sumptuous East India House
at Amsterdam in 1638, Joost van den Vondel, the greatest
of Dutch poets, celebrated the occasion with an ode
rhapsodising the commercial enterprise of his countrymen
in the Orient, whose driving motive he thus expressed in
his concluding lines:

> Wherever profit leads us, to every sea and shore
> For love of gain the wide world's harbours we explore.

"Love of gain" was indeed the compelling reason that
brought the Dutch traders to the East, as it brought the
Portuguese long before them, and the English very soon
after them—and the original objective of all three nations
was trade, not territory. With Portuguese expansion we
are not concerned here; but just as the "cheese-mongers of

[1] [Copyright © C. R. Boxer. Originally published in *History Today*, VIII (1958), pp. 145-54.]

Leadenhall Street" gradually became lords of a territorial
empire in the Indian sub-continent after Robert Clive's
intervention in the Carnatic and Bengal, so the Directors
of the Dutch East-India Company unwittingly took the
first steps towards unifying Indonesia and conquering Java
when they gave belated approval to Cornelis Speelman's
forceful intervention in the affairs of Macassar, Mataram,
and Bantam. Admittedly, the circumstances leading to
Clive's intervention on the one hand and to that of
Speelman on the other were very different: but if Clive is
considered to be one of the founders of the British Empire
in India, then Speelman can be cast for a similar role in
the history of the Dutch in Indonesia.

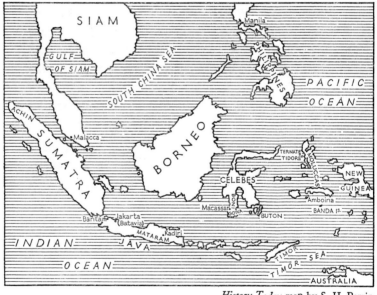

History Today map by S. H. Perrin

The East Indies

When the Europeans arrived in the islands of the Malay Archipelago there was no political—or religious—feeling of Indonesian unity, and neither the sixteenth-century Portuguese pioneers nor their seventeenth-century Dutch successors strove to implant it. After the collapse of the Hinduised empire of Majapahit—concerning whose power and extent scholars still differ widely—round about 1530, Java was roughly divided between various trading principalities on the coast and the agrarian states in the interior, which eventually coalesced into the Islamised empire of Mataram. In North Sumatra, Muslim Achin held European Malacca in check, though it could not prevent the Westerners from trading with the petty pepper-producing kingdoms of the south and west. Endemic strife between the rival sultans of Ternate and Tidore in the Moluccan Spice Islands greatly facilitated the successive establishment of the Portuguese, Spaniards, and Dutch in that region: but European influence elsewhere was negligible, save in a negative sense. The militant Roman Catholicism of the Portuguese and the rigidly intolerant Calvinism of the Dutch, alike, provoked as a reaction the spread of Islam throughout the island world of Indonesia. Whereas the Muslim faith had previously been confined to the harbour states, it was now taken up in the interior of Java, although both princes and people retained a large measure of their former Hindu and of their still older animistic beliefs.

Jan Pieterszoon Coen (Governor-General 1618-23 and 1627-9) is usually regarded as the real founder of the Dutch empire in the East, though he did not—except for a short time—visualise the establishment of a territorial empire,

E.E.—D

but of a maritime and commercial one, something after the Portuguese pattern. He hoped to use Dutch naval superiority in such a way as to crush all European and Asian competitors in the seaborne trade of Asia, and to finance the East-India Company's trade with Europe from the expected profits of Dutch domination of the Asian interport trade. In pursuance of this policy, he drove the English from the Spice Islands, whence the Portuguese had been expelled two decades earlier, and founded Dutch Batavia on the site of the Javanese Jakarta[2] as a "general rendezvous" and entrepot for the maritime trade of Asia. This—and it was already much—was the limit of his success, for his plans were too far-reaching to be practicable. Although the Dutch were believed to have more shipping at their disposal than the rest of Europe put together, they certainly had not got enough to monopolise the seaborne trade of Asia from the Red Sea to Japan. Coen failed to take the two Iberian bulwarks of Macao and Manila on the shores of the South China Sea, and he died in Batavia, closely—though unsuccessfully—invested by a huge Javanese army from Mataram.

Coen's plans were adapted on a more modest and more successful scale by Antonio van Diemen. During his ten years of office (1636-45) he broke the power of the Portuguese, and strengthened the Dutch grip on the Spice Islands by methods which, if not quite so drastic as Coen's extirpation of the Banda islanders, at any rate involved cutting off heads as well as cutting down surplus clove-trees on a considerable scale. His work was largely

[2] Which resumed its old name with the proclamation of Indonesian independence after World War II.

completed by Rijkloff van Goens, who in the years 1658-63 drove the Portuguese from their remaining settlements in Ceylon and Malabar. Though now firmly established as the strongest maritime power in Asia, the Dutch East-India Company was still not a territorial power, save in the lowlands of Ceylon and in the unfrequented hinterland of the Cape of Good Hope. Formosa, which had bid fair to become a flourishing colony as well as an entrepot for the China-Japan trade in the time of Van Diemen and his immediate successors, had been taken by Chinese partisans of the fallen Ming dynasty in 1662. The remaining Dutch settlements were either small islands or coastal forts and "factories" (trading agencies) where their control did not extend beyond the range of their guns.

On Java, their foothold at Batavia was only a small enclave wedged between the great empire of Mataram, which under Sultan Amangkurat I (1645-77) extended over three-quarters of the island, and the smaller but still formidable sultanate of Bantam in the western corner. Of the other major Indonesian kingdoms, Ternate, with its vague suzerainty over the Moluccas, was already a client-state or "satellite" of the Dutch; while the power of Achin in Sumatra was obviously declining after the death of the great Sultan Iskander Muda (1636). Their most dangerous rival was undoubtedly the rising Muslim sultanate of Macassar in the South Celebes, whose able rulers were resolved not to recognise the Dutch monopoly of the Moluccan spice trade, and whose adventurous seafaring subjects, "the fighting-cocks of the East", gave the Dutch endless trouble in Amboina and elsewhere. The monopoly of the spice-trade was described as the "right arm" of the Dutch commercial system in Asia; and as long as the Macassar interlopers continued their activities that monopoly was never really effective. The rulers of Macassar also made a point of patronising and encouraging the Portuguese, English, and Danish competitors of the Dutch, and the first-named had a large and flourishing settlement there. Several of the leading Macassar nobles were remarkably fluent in Portuguese and Spanish, and at least two possessed excellent libraries of European books. One of these men had read all the works of Fr. Luis de Granada O.P., a famous Spanish devotional writer, in the original, and Vondel wrote an ode extolling his geographical knowledge.

The Directors of the East-India Company in Holland more than once stressed their desire for peaceful as well as profitable trade in Asia, and their aversion to a mailed-fist policy, particularly in areas where the Dutch had no forts and no special treaty-rights. In the standing-orders for the Governor-General and his council elaborated in 1650, the Directors specifically enjoined their subordinates at Batavia "always to keep in view the necessity of peaceful trade throughout all Asia, from which is derived the smoke in the kitchens here at home". Despite their own efforts to monopolise the spice-trade of the Moluccas, they stressed that "the Company's trade all over the Indies must be based on the common right of all peoples, consisting in freedom of commerce", and they forbade the use of force save only in the very few places that were under the Company's direct control.

These peaceful injunctions did not always fall on receptive ears at Batavia. Rijkloff van Goens, the conqueror of Ceylon and Malabar, spoke for others besides himself when he told the Directors five years later that:

> The Christian maxims which Your Honours have continually had before you, to pursue trade and commerce with all the Asian powers in peace and friendship, are misunderstood by them. For there are none in Asia who wish us well, yea we are in truth deadly hated by all nations—because even if we try to win over each one with justice, moderation, and uprightness, yet each one of them is resolved to ruin us, . . . so I feel that sooner or later war will be the ultimate arbiter.

The final showdown with Sultan Hassan Udin of Macassar began in October 1666, when the Governor-General and council at Batavia, without reference to the Directors in Holland, resolved to send a strong expedition to South Celebes to forestall an allegedly intended attack by Macassar on Ternate.

Command of this expedition was given to Cornelis Speelman, whose character and career deserve a brief mention, in view of the prominent part that he played in the disintegration of three of the major Indonesian states in the ensuing years. Born in March 1628, the son of a prosperous burgher family of Rotterdam, he sailed for Java at the age of sixteen, and though he sometimes declared his intention to return home, the rest of his life was spent in Asia. His first important post was as Secretary to a Dutch embassy to Persia in 1651-2, of which he wrote a detailed account, including one of the earliest descriptions of the ruins of Persepolis. In 1663-5, he was Governor of the Dutch possessions on the Coromandel Coast, where he was on suspiciously friendly terms with the rascally Governor of Madras, Sir Edward Winter. The rest of his service had been spent at Batavia, where he was famous as a genial toper in a community of deep drinkers, styling himself "the great Professor of Bacchus' pupils". He might have added "and of Venus", since his contemporaries assure us that he was also "a great lover of women". His long-suffering wife finally left (though she did not divorce) him, "because so many children on the streets of Batavia bore such a striking resemblance to him".

But, although he frequently drank his boon companions under the table, these night-long debauches did not prevent him from working up to sixteen hours the next day in the stifling atmosphere of Batavia Castle. He often dictated three different dispatches at once, and he audited the most complicated accounts with a speed and thoroughness that a modern income tax collector might envy. He also spoke fluent Malay and made a close study of the traditions, manners, and customs of the principal Asian races with whom he came into contact in Java, Coromandel and Celebes. Despite burning the candle at both ends, his remarkable constitution for long seemed quite unaffected by his excessive zest for work and play. It may be added that he died a millionaire; not so much because he was in any case well-to-do, and had originally married a rich wife, as because he acted as moneylender on a large scale to Chinese and Indonesian merchants.

It took Speelman nearly three years of hard, if inter-mittent, fighting to break the strength and the spirit of the "fighting-cocks of the East". He never disposed of more than a few hundred European soldiers, and the bulk of his expeditionary force consisted of Indonesian auxiliary troops, chiefly Ambonese, with a large contingent of Buginese warriors led by their exiled Prince, Aru Palacca of Boni, who was a personal friend of Speelman. The kingdom of Boni adjoined that of Gowa, the homeland of the Sultans of Macassar, and had been conquered by the latter a few years previously. Several of Aru Palacca's relatives had been killed on that occasion and he was now a fugitive seeking revenge. His people rose *en masse* to join him when the Dutch brought him back; and this proved the decisive factor in the hard-fought campaign. Just as the Spanish conquest of the Philippines was facilitated by the support they received from the Pampangos and Tagalos, and the British conquest of India by the Sepoy regiments, so the Dutch subjugation of Macassar, and later of Mataram, was only rendered practicable because of the help they received from other Indonesian peoples.

Speelman's first move was to corner a Macassar force of 15,000 men on the island of Buton, where they were attacking the local ruler, who was an ally of the East-India Company. Nearly half of them were conscripted Buginese, who either deserted before the Macassar commander capitulated or else took service with Aru Palacca after the surrender. There was considerable discussion among the victors as to what to do with the remaining Macassar prisoners, who totalled over five thousand. The Sultan of Buton was for killing them out of hand, but Speelman declined to do this: "To kill in cold blood men who have laid down their arms and come to surrender unconditionally—that is going too far!" he exclaimed. The upshot, however, was much the same. Four hundred

picked men and women were sent to be sold as slaves in
the Moluccas, where, wrote Speelman, the Chinese "and
others" would give a good price for "the numerous pretty
women" who were included in that number. The remaining five thousand were marooned on a neglected islet
with a small supply of rice. With the exception of a few
strong swimmers who reached the coast of Celebes
through shark-infested waters, these poor wretches all
died of hunger and malnutrition within a few weeks, and
the islet has since borne the name of Pulo Macassar.

After picking up fresh Indonesian auxiliaries at Ternate,
Speelman returned to South Celebes and launched a frontal
attack on Gowa, with the co-operation of Aru Palacca
and the Buginese from the landward side. After four
months of hard fighting, Sultan Hassan Udin asked for
terms, and Speelman dictated the so-called Treaty of
Bongaja, which was duly ratified by the Sultan's emis-
saries at Batavia in March 1668. But when it came to
enforcing the onerous stipulations of this Treaty, which
reduced Macassar to complete dependence on the Company and restored Boni to Aru Palacca, the "fighting-cocks
of the East" put up another desperate struggle before they
were finally subdued after an even tougher campaign.
It was typical of Speelman that during these two campaigns, and in spite of being racked by recurrent bouts
of kidney trouble and malarial fever, he found time to
compile a report on the political and social conditions in
South Celebes which totalled over 800 folio pages.

The subjugation of South Celebes and the construction
at Macassar of a Dutch castle, which Speelman christened
"Rotterdam" after his birthplace, closed the last loophole

in the Dutch monopoly of the Moluccan spice-trade, which now became virtually one hundred per cent effective. The other European traders, who were driven from Macassar, found a refuge at Bantam, where their compatriots had long been well established: but Bantam, though an important pepper-trading and shipping centre, was not nearly so well placed as Macassar for interfering in the Moluccas. As I have mentioned previously, the power of Achin was already in decline; and that decline was now accelerated by Dutch military intervention in Western Sumatra. Various petty principalities were here transferred from Achinese suzerainty to that of the Company, mainly with the aid of Aru Palacca, Captain Joncker,[3] and the Buginese and Ambonese auxiliaries who had helped to conquer Macassar.

The seemingly powerful Javanese kingdoms of Mataram and Bantam had not hitherto been radically affected by the establishment of the Dutch at Batavia; and neither the Directors in the Netherlands nor their cautious Governor-General in the East-Indies, Johan Maetsuyker (1653-78), had shown any desire to interfere in the internal affairs of these two states. They were satisfied as long as Mataram and Bantam did not combine together against Batavia, but kept each other roughly in balance through their rivalry for the overlordship of the whole island. Speelman, however, had more ambitious views and his chance came in 1676-8. In those years a civil war over the crown of Mataram led the defeated claimant—who was also, conveniently, the legitimate heir—to appeal to the Dutch at Batavia to restore him to his throne. This

[3] A full-blooded Ambonese despite his Dutch *nom de guerre*.

took longer than expected as the majority of his subjects
sided with the Madurese usurper, and Governor-General
Maetsuyker was loath to let the impetuous Speelman, who
was nominated "admiral and commander-in-chief", carry
out his plan of marching straight on the Mataram capital
of Kadiri and reinstating the Susuhunan[4]; there. In fact,
Maetsuyker's caution was so excessive that Speelman once
retorted sarcastically: "The only objection I miss in your
letter is that perhaps even the sky will fall down from
heaven and destroy the whole human race".

At the beginning of 1678 Maetsuyker died and was
succeeded by the more aggressive Rijkloff van Goens.
Speelman was recalled to Batavia and installed as Director-
General, the next senior position in the Dutch East-India
Company's official hierarchy, and he promptly used his
influence to have the war prosecuted with greater vigour.
Kadiri was duly occupied, and the legitimate Susuhunan
reinstated—after a Dutch officer had tactlessly tried the
sacred crown on his own head—but he was a weak and
wenching character who was nothing more than a Dutch
puppet. The Dutch imposed their own terms, which,
while leaving the administration entirely in Javanese
hands, gave them a monopoly of Mataram's foreign trade.
They also secured the cession of a broad belt of territory
running due south from Batavia across the Preanger
highlands to the sea. Here again the Buginese and other
auxiliaries of the Dutch played a leading part in the conquest of Mataram. It was Aru Palacca's Buginese who
garrisoned Batavia while many of the Europeans were

4 "He to whom everything is subject", title taken by the Sultans
of Mataram since 1625.

away; and it was Captain Joncker's Ambonese who finally ran the usurper to earth in the jungle-covered mountains of East Java. True to form, it was also in the intervals of this strenuous campaign that Speelman compiled a bulky folio description of Mataram which rivalled his previous encyclopaedic account of Macassar.

In some ways, perhaps, the downfall of Mataram was less important than that of Bantam. The former was never a sea-power and its seventeenth-century sultans were tyrannical oriental despots of a conventional kind. They did not concern themselves with commerce, but with women, hunting, and war; and, provided the Dutch recognised their over-lordship, they did not greatly care if Batavia monopolised the foreign trade of their subjects. Sultan Agung (1651-83) of Bantam, on the other hand, like the rulers of Macassar, strongly resented Dutch pretensions to commercial monopoly, and he tried to turn his capital into an entrepot that would rival Batavia. He sent two ambassadors to England, who received rather unflattering mention in Evelyn's *Diary* under 19 Jun. 1682: "They were both very hard-favoured, and much resembling in countenance some sort of monkeys," though he added grudgingly: "They were very sober, and I believe subtle in their way." Sultan Agung also encouraged Chinese, Arabian, and Indonesian traders as well as the European rivals of the Dutch, and his own ships sailed as far as the Philippines and the Red Sea.

In Bantam, as in Mataram, a succession-dispute played into Dutch hands. Speelman, who had succeeded Van Goens as Governor-General in 1681, seized the opportunity thus afforded him. Sultan Agung's eldest son,

known as Haji on account of his pilgrimage to Mecca, fell
out with his father when the old man tried to resume the
throne shortly after he had abdicated in his favour. As
most of the people supported the father in the ensuing
civil war, Sultan Haji appealed to Speelman for help. The
Governor-General promptly obliged: but in return the
sultan was forced to expel the English and other foreign
traders, to grant the Dutch Company a monopoly of the
pepper and textile trades, and to cede a portion of his
territory. Speelman's remarkable constitution had been
gradually undermined by recurrent attacks of kidney and
liver trouble ever since the Macassar campaign, and he
died a few months before the Bantam Treaty was signed
in April 1684. But he died secure in the knowledge that
his work was done, and the Dutch fort which symbolised
their domination at Bantam was appropriately called
Speelwyk in his honour.

It is often supposed in England that, after the "massacre
of Amboina" in 1623, the English withdrew entirely from
Indonesia to concentrate their efforts in India proper,
whereas the Dutch devoted virtually all their attention to
the Malay Archipelago and paid little heed to the regions
west of the straits of Malacca. This is a serious miscon-
ception. If the Moluccan spice-trade was the "right arm"
of the Dutch East-India Company, the Indian textile
trade was avowedly its left; and, down to the end of the
seventeenth century at least, the Dutch position in the
Indian Ocean was much more imposing than that of the
British. Whereas in 1670 the fortified English possessions
in Hindustan were confined to Bombay and Madras, the
Dutch had a string of fortified settlements on the Malabar

and Coromandel coasts, and their establishment at
Chinsurah in Bengal considerably antedated our Fort
William at Calcutta. They controlled the whole of the
Ceylon littoral, and their trade with the Persian Gulf and
the Red Sea rivalled that of the English. The influential
Rijkloff van Goens repeatedly advocated the conquest of
Raja Sinha's highland kingdom of Kandy in Ceylon, with
the object of turning the whole island into a Dutch colony
and making Colombo, instead of Batavia, the seat of
their eastern empire. One of the foremost opponents of
Van Goens' plan was Cornelis Speelman, and it was his
view, which favoured expansion in Indonesia, that prevailed. The concentration of the Dutch on the Indonesian
sector of their commercial empire dates not from 1623,
but from the downfall of Macassar, Mataram, and Bantam
in 1666-84.

The conquest of Java and the unification of Indonesia
by the Dutch were not accomplished in a generation, any
more than Clive's spectacular victories in the Carnatic
and Bengal meant that the English East-India Company
had become the paramount power in Hindustan by 1765.
The establishment of the British Raj had to wait until after
the partition of Mysore (1799) and the defeat of the
Maratha Confederacy (1819); and even then the Sikh
Wars and the Indian Mutiny remained to be fought.
Similarly, the Dutch had to fight three succession-wars
and partition Maratam during the eighteenth century,
and to contend with Dipa Negoro's insurrection of 1825-
30, before their hold on the island was really secure. Their
conquest of Achin and of the outer islands had to wait
even longer; and it was not finally completed until the

beginning of the present century. But just as, after Clive and Plassey, there was perforce no looking back once the English East-India Company had become the *de facto* rulers of Bengal, so, with the conquests made by Cornelis Speelman, the Dutch East-India Company unwittingly began the unification of Indonesia.

J. W. Davidson

PETER DILLON AND THE
SOUTH SEAS[1]

Like waves breaking on Pacific shores, each one over-
taken by the next before its energy is quite spent, the
phases of Pacific history have followed one another,
merging and over-lapping. In the first phase, the expansion of geographical knowledge was the primary motive
for the Europeans' intrusion. Then, before the work of
discovery was quite done, traders, whalers, settlers, and
missionaries came to the islands, to be followed, in their
turn, by the agents of Western political control.

The times of mergence, when one phase of development lost momentum and was over-laid by its successor,
are often marked with dramatic force. So it is that the
end of the age of exploration can be placed on 14 Feb.
1779, when Captain Cook was killed on the island of
Hawaii. The voyages of Cook and his immediate predecessors, Byron, Wallis, Carteret, and Bougainville, had
laid bare the main outlines of Pacific geography. Basing
their work upon the accumulated knowledge of earlier

[1] [Copyright © J. W. Davidson. Originally published in *History
Today*, VI (1956), pp. 307-17.]

voyagers, they had destroyed the hypothesis of a southern continent, defined the eastern coast of Australia and, in less detail, the north-west coast of America, charted New Zealand (first briefly seen by Tasman over a century before), discovered many island groups (including the Society Islands and Hawaii), and supplied much detailed information about places, like Tonga and the New Hebrides, of which previous knowledge had been fragmentary and inexact. And to their work of surveying they had added careful study of the peoples and the products of the Pacific.

After Cook's death there was, indeed, still a vast body of geographical work to be done. Large tracts of ocean remained untraversed; many coastlines were only roughly charted; the position of innumerable islands had to be verified, and even their existence proved; and winds and tides and ocean currents needed careful study. But knowledge was sufficient to entice others than explorers into the Pacific and to enable them to sail its waters in relative safety. Within a few years, the masters of merchant ships, using the narratives of the explorers in place of formal pilot books, were entering many of its harbours. About 1785 British merchants began to trade for furs on the American north-west coast; in 1787 Lieutenant William Bligh was sent to Tahiti in the *Bounty* to procure breadfruit trees for transplantation to the West Indies; in 1788 Captain Arthur Phillip arrived at Sydney cove; in 1796 British whalers, which had already been working off the coast of Chile, began to come westward to Polynesia and the Australian coast; in 1797 the (London) Missionary Society landed missionaries in Tahiti, the Marquesas, and

Tonga. The Pacific was being drawn steadily within the confines of the Western world.

By the early years of the nineteenth century, trade was beginning between Europeans and natives in many island groups. The fur-traders were calling at Hawaii, and the whalers were putting into many of the islands between New Zealand and the Equator for fresh food and water. In 1801 and the following years Governor King, of New South Wales, sent vessels to Tahiti, to trade for pork and to show the Tahitians the benefits of commerce. This venture succeeded in both its objects, but it had a further result: it aroused the interest of Sydney merchants in the possibilities of South Sea islands trade. Just as the excitement of the first voyages to Tahiti was subsiding, the chance came for the merchants to experiment. In 1804 it became known in Sydney that sandalwood had been discovered in Fiji. Known supplies, in Malabar and Timor, were very limited. The main demand was in China, where it was highly valued for its fragrance and was burned in temples, mixed with cosmetics, and used for making articles such as fans. Those who were told the location of "Sandal Wood Bay" (Mbua Bay, in Vanua Levu) sent out vessels and hoped to keep their knowledge to themselves. But the secret did not survive the first voyages. In 1807 a general rush began. Ships sailed for Fiji from India and America, as well as from New South Wales.

On one of the Indian vessels there arrived in 1808 a young seaman, Peter Dillon. An Irish Catholic, with little education, he came from a background not dissimilar to that of many who sought their livings at sea; but already, at the age of 20, he stood out as an individual.

E.E.——E

He was six feet four in height, heavily built, with a mop of red hair. His manner was self-confident, even arrogant. His mind was acute, his sense of humour ribald and boisterous. When aroused to anger, he lashed his adversaries indiscriminately with a vicious tongue, fists, or any weapon within reach. But in time of danger he was calm and efficient. And, most significantly, he lacked any sense of superiority in his relations with native peoples. From the start, he found the Fijians as deserving of respect as men of his own race. Patiently and intelligently, he set to work to learn their language and to understand their culture. In Fiji he left his ship. Probably he deserted or was dismissed after a dispute. On shore he took some part in obtaining at least one cargo of sandalwood—£15,000-worth in three weeks, he later claimed. But his main interest was in the Fijians. The chiefs, the young women, the children—all, in their different ways, were his friends. His influence grew, and soon the traders were alleging that he was persuading the Fijians to demand higher pay for their labour.

After four months he embarked on a trading vessel for Sydney. He seems to have gone back to Fiji on a short visit early in the following year. After that, he took part in the trade to the Society Islands. Late in 1808 he sailed as a seaman on Wills and Reibey's vessel, the *Mercury*, for Tahiti, *via* New Zealand. On his return, he was signed on again by the same firm, as mate or supercargo. And, on this occasion, he remained for over a year in the Society Islands procuring cargoes of salt pork. It gave him time, as in Fiji, to learn a language and become absorbed into a Pacific island's society. He was adopted by

a relative of the chief Pomare. This was the most critical
period in Pomare's career. Following the example of his
father, who had been the friend of Cook and Bligh,
Pomare had determined to become the king of all Tahiti
and of its neighbouring islands, with the aid of European
weapons and advice. The missionaries had become his
allies; the traders had sold him muskets in exchange for
pork. But, inevitably, there was a reaction on the part of
those at whose expense his ambition was being realised.

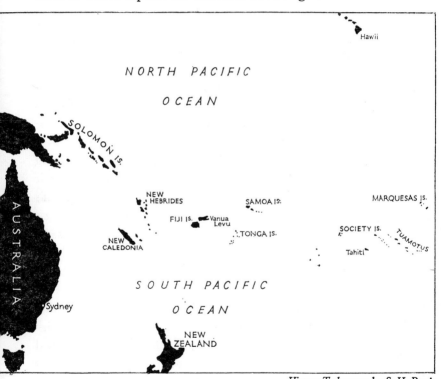

History Today map by S. H. Perrin

The South Seas

Several years before, he had been forced to flee from Tahiti to the neighbouring island of Moorea; and most of the missionaries had been frightened by the ensuing disorder into sailing on a trading vessel to New South Wales. But now the tide was again turning; and Pomare's friendly relations with Europeans were the factor that established his success. For Dillon, his presence in the Society Islands at this time created ties of friendship and affection that were broken only by death.

After his return to Sydney, Dillon travelled to Norfolk Island. He was there in December 1812, when the ship *Hunter*, Captain Robson, of Calcutta, called at the island *en route* to Fiji. His acceptance of the post of third officer led him into one of the crucial adventures of his life. Robson had paid two previous visits to Fiji and, according to Dillon, "had obtained considerable influence over the natives of a part of the Sandal-wood coast, by joining them in their wars, and assisting them to destroy their enemies, who were cut up, baked, and eaten in his presence". On this occasion also he sought to increase his popularity (and so obtain a better cargo) in the same way. Robson's men helped their native allies at Wailea to kill their enemies and to destroy their "towns and plantations". But eventually—with the over-confidence so common among Europeans in the Pacific since that first voyage on which Magellan had paid for his rashness with his life—they dared too much. "May, June, July, and August passed over," Dillon declares, "and we had only procured one hundred and fifty tons of sandal-wood from the islanders, which was not more than one-third of a cargo. They then declared their inability to procure more . . . " Robson was furious at what he believed to be dishonest evasion by his allies of their debt to him for help in their wars. He decided to treat them as he had their enemies. He attacked the Wailea canoe fleet and followed this up with an attack on land. The angry Fijians fought back with vigour and success. The chief mate and several other Europeans in the attacking force were killed. Dillon then took command of the survivors and led them to a high rock where they would be safe from enemy spears and slings. The problem now was to make their ammunition last till they could find a way of escape. Dillon insisted that no shot should be fired till an attacker was within point-blank range. By adopting this course, one man is said to have killed 27 Fijians with 28 shots. Even so, as Dillon knew, they were merely buying time. On the flat below them, fires were burning on which, as the Fijians jeeringly told them, their bodies were to be cooked that evening. Dillon opened discussions as to the conditions on which they would come down from the rock. A priest was allowed to climb up to them. Then Dillon seized his chance; he stuck his musket against the man's head and, thus, walking behind the priest, led his little band to liberty.

Those on board the *Hunter* now included a German, Martin Buchert, and a lascar, both of whom had been living in Fiji, and three Fijian women who had been "wives" of Europeans. It was obviously impossible for them to land again at Wailea. They were therefore placed on board a small cutter accompanying the *Hunter*, the *Elizabeth*, which was now under Dillon's command,

and the two men and one of the women were eventually landed on the island of Tikopia, on the outskirts of the Solomons. It was a chance action whose consequences were to bring Dillon, many years later, the greatest triumph of his career. Now, at Tikopia, the two vessels parted: the *Hunter*, under Robson, sailed for India; the *Elizabeth*, under Dillon, for New South Wales.

In Sydney, the story of Dillon's recent adventure in Fiji quickly became known, and he soon found employment suitable to his talents. For several years past, the Rev. Samuel Marsden had been trying to establish a settlement of the Church Missionary Society in New Zealand. He had obtained the Society's approval of the venture during a trip to England in 1807; but, while he was on his way back to Australia in 1809, the *Boyd* massacre occurred at Whangaroa. Until 1814 the scheme had been held up. Marsden, however, now decided to despatch a preliminary expedition to negotiate with the Maoris at the Bay of Islands: but, as he later wrote, he "felt at a loss to find a suitable person to navigate the brig, because [of] the risk of being murdered and eaten. . . . Mr Dillon . . . was then in Sydney (1814), and I engaged him to take command of the *Active*". In March, Dillon sailed, with two of the prospective mission settlers, Thomas Kendall and William Hall, and a Maori named Tuhi. According to the over-sensitive Kendall, the expedition had many moments of friction. But, by less subjective standards, it was an undoubted success. Negotiations with the Maoris had been conducted with skill and sympathy. In Marsden's reticent words "Mr. Dillon sailed with the missionaries, and in due time returned to Port Jackson without injury to himself, the crew, nor to the vessel."

For Dillon, the return to Sydney was more than the end of a job. A month later, he was married at St Philip's Church to Mary Moore, the daughter of a Sydney box-maker. For the time being, his marriage cut him off from a life of adventure among the islands. At first he took jobs on coastal vessels. Then, in 1816, he sailed with his wife and infant son for Calcutta. He found employment there in the Indian "country trade". For three years he served as an officer and gained a wide knowledge of the Eastern Seas. Then, in 1819, he acquired a ship of his own. In her he sailed from Calcutta, with a cargo of foodstuffs, clothing, liquor, and other merchandise for the Australian colonies. The venture was apparently profitable, for he made two further voyages of the same kind. On the third, in July 1823, he sailed from Sydney for Chile to pick up a return cargo—of wheat, tobacco, wine, and copper—for the colonies and Calcutta. At this time, Valparaiso was something of a boom town; and, when he arrived there, Dillon joined with a local merchant in buying a second vessel, which they named the *St Patrick*, and sent her to New Zealand for a cargo of *kauri* spars. Meanwhile, in the *Calder*, he sailed for Callao, in Peru. His main object was certainly commercial: but he never allowed his pur-suit of fortune to dim his other interests. In Pacific history, one of the mysteries which had always puzzled him was the evidence of two Spanish visits there. It seemed, too, that Roman Catholic ceremonies had been performed on shore. What had been the purpose of the visitors and whence had they come? Cook himself had wondered; so had the missionaries, and so had Dillon. Now report reached him that in the neighbouring city of Lima there was an old woman still living whose husband had gone on those two voyages. He sought her out. The riddle was largely solved. In the spring of 1772, the Viceroy, Don Manuel de Amat, had despatched the frigate *Aguila* from Callao. She had been at Tahiti for a month, in November and December, and had then returned to Peru. In 1774 the *Aguila*, this time accompanied by another vessel, the *Jupiter*, had sailed again. On this occasion two priests with their attendants were landed and left in Tahiti for about a year. It was the widow of one of these attendants, Máximo Rodriguez, the interpreter, whom Dillon met. She possessed a copy of a diary kept by her husband. Dillon obtained a transcript of it; and, in due course, published a summary in Calcutta.

On his return to Valparaiso, he prepared the *Calder* for another voyage; and in the winter of 1824 he sailed, nominally "in search of sandalwood". In fact, he was embarking on the kind of enterprise which delighted him, one in which there was little profit in terms of money, but much in terms of experience. With the narratives of the explorers open before him, he lived again the lives of Wallis, of Bougainville, of Cook. He followed the movements of sun and stars, inhaled the breezes blown off island shores with the concentration and excitement of the Polynesian navigators of many centuries before or of their successors who were now bent upon the extension of Christianity through the eastern archipelagoes. Between the Tuamotus, east of Tahiti, and New Caledonia, in the west, he visited innumerable islands. He spent some time with his old friends in Tahiti; he exchanged ideas about the Pacific with missionaries like John Williams; he took on board, at Tongatapu, as passengers, a Fijian chief and his Tongan friend; he returned again to "Sandal Wood Bay" in Fiji. Then, he writes, "I sailed . . . late in January (1825) for the New Hebrides, and in a few days anchored at Port Resolution in the Island of Tanna. It appeared to me that no ship had been there since Captain Cook left it." He found "a few of the old natives" who could pronounce that "memorable name" and those of Wales and Forster. On Tana, he found a few pieces of sandalwood, and, in answer to enquiries, he learnt that on the neighbouring island of Eromanga there was abundance. He made little use of the discovery himself, but as a result of it most of the sandalwood trade of the Pacific eventually centred upon the New Hebrides.

After visits to New Caledonia and New Zealand, he returned to Sydney. His mind and conversation were filled with knowledge and impressions of the Pacific. He talked of Mendaña, of Quiros, of Cook, of Polynesian canoe voyages. He spoke with sympathy and acuteness about the cultural differences between the various peoples he had been amongst, noting, for example, that the Fijians alone made pottery. But he enjoyed most of all, probably, the introduction of his Fijian and Tongan passengers to Sydney society. On all his Pacific voyages he picked up some of his Polynesian friends, took them to distant cities, and returned them to their homes loaded with gifts.

After only a month, Dillon sailed again for Valparaiso where he set to work at once acquiring a cargo of "wheat, wine, flour, plums, raisins, almonds, tobacco, &c. &c.", for New South Wales. But before the *Calder* was loaded, she was driven ashore in a gale. In this extremity, Dillon bought his partner's share in the *St Patrick*, which had returned from New Zealand with a highly profitable cargo of spars. He determined to load spars in New Zealand again, this time for Calcutta. The "trade" from the *Calder* was transferred; muskets—perhaps used already in the Chilean War of Independence—and gunpowder were bought; and some horses and donkeys were loaded for Tahiti. The ship's company (except for some South Sea Islanders) were all entered as "naturalized Chilians" from "Don Pedro Dillon, capitán primero" downwards; and with the Chilian colours at the peak and "an enormous green flag with yellow Irish harp in it" at the main, they sailed out of Valparaiso.

Three luxurious weeks were spent at Tahiti. One day, records George Bayly, the third mate, Queen Pomare (daughter of the former King) and the Royal Family came aboard.

> They were received with a salute of musketry, and escorted down to the state-room. Here I was instructed to exhibit all our treasures. They took a great fancy to the Jew's-harps, and Peter (he was only known by his Christian name amongst these islands) at once presented one to each of them, and showed the way to use them. Their Royal Highnesses all squatted down with their backs to the bulkhead and their harps at their lips, making all manner of faces in their vain attempts to follow the captain's instructions. Peter meanwhile sat

on the table with a large Jew's-harp, and twanged away
at some lively Irish jig, whilst the queen, princes, and
princesses continually burst into roars of laughter at the
sight of each other's grimaces. . . .

From Tahiti they sailed south towards New Zealand,
calling at various islands on the way. On 31 Dec. 1825
they cast anchor in the New Zealand River Thames,
where Dillon at once made a contract with Maori chiefs
for the supply of spars.

After nearly four months on the New Zealand coast,
they resumed their voyage. Then, "on my way . . . towards
Bengal", writes Dillon, "I came in sight of Tucopia on
the morning of the 13th May". It was the island on which,
thirteen years before, he had landed three survivors of the
affray in Fiji. Canoes came out, and in them were the
German, Buchert, and the lascar. With him the lascar
brought a silver sword-guard. At sight of it Dillon's eyes
were aglow with eagerness. Where had it been obtained?
What other European articles were possesssed by the
Tikopians? The story was soon told: "when the old men
now in Tucopia were boys", two large ships had been
wrecked on the island of Vanikoro; the lascar had been
there in a canoe; he had seen large quantities of wreckage;
he had talked with two survivors. Could there be any
doubt as to the discovery Dillon had stumbled upon?

As Dillon and George Bayly had worked together on
the *St Patrick* making musket cartridges to sell to the
Maoris, sometimes Dillon had told him the extraordinary
adventures of his own life, and sometimes Bayly had
read aloud from the voyages of the early navigators. On
these occasions Dillon had shown his interest in the

strange and tragic story of La Pérouse; and he had con-
fessed to the desire he had cherished for years to solve
the mystery. In 1785 Jean François Galaup de la Pérouse
had sailed from France; in 1786 and 1787 he had carried
out valuable and skilful surveys of the North American
and Asian coasts; and then he had sailed south through
Polynesia to Botany Bay, where the first shiploads of
convicts had recently arrived. From the coast of New
South Wales he went north again intent on solving the
one great geographical puzzle of the South Pacific—the
identity of Mendaña's Solomon Islands. Then there was
silence. Neither he nor his expedition had been heard of
again. The disappearance of this brilliant and much be-
loved man had grieved his contemporaries and mystified
his successors. In 1791 the French Constituent Assembly
voted a reward to anyone throwing light on the mystery;
and an expedition was despatched under Bruni d'Entrecasteaux to make an organised search. But d'Entrecasteaux
failed; and for over thirty years not a shred of evidence
had been found. Now the ocean was at last yielding up its
long-hidden secret: La Pérouse's ships had been cast
away on Vanikoro. The more Dillon wracked his brain
for alternative explanations of what he had just heard, the
more certain he became of the truth of his first surmise.
Taking Buchert on board they sailed that evening towards
the west, but winds hindered them; and the leaky state
of the ship and the shortage of provisions forced them to
give up the search and hasten towards India.

Dillon landed at Calcutta at the end of August 1826
to tell his story. He communicated it to the government
of Bengal and urged the necessity of sending an expedi-

tion to Vanikoro without delay. He declared his own intention of carrying out this project if he were able. It was found, however, that the *St Patrick* needed extensive repairs. Dillon first suggested that the authorities might lend him the money to have these carried out; but it was eventually decided that one of the Company's own vessels, the *Research*, should be made ready and Dillon placed in command of her. His own enthusiasm had carried the day. And he was equally successful in obtaining the support of the French authorities at Chandernagore. In his desire to ensure approval he even told, and effectively persuaded, the naval officer in command there that he was a Frenchman (though he spoke no French). A representative of the French government was appointed to the expedition. In January 1827 the *Research* sailed from the Hooghly.

On this voyage George Bayly had declined to go. Young, intelligent, able to share in Dillon's interest in exploration and to act for him as a kind of secretary, he was apparently a favourite with him. But nothing could efface his memories of Dillon's violence. In the private account of his experiences on the *Calder* and the *St Patrick*, which he wrote shortly afterwards, he noted: "Captain Dillon was the most passionate man I ever saw. His wife lived on board and he very frequently gave her a thrashing, sometimes striking her to the deck, and once broke his telescope to pieces about her head." He tells of axes and other implements being thrown at members of the ship's company who had aroused Dillon's wrath. And he describes the solemn and steady persecution of the clumsy steward. Dillon wrote the single word "Crimes" at the top of a sheet of paper and the numbers 1 to 12 down the side. When the number was made up, the steward was flogged. On this occasion, there were signs that Dillon's temper would be put to a more than ordinary test. Before they sailed, Tytler, the surgeon, probably wishing to obtain command of the expedition for himself, had tried to have Dillon certified as insane. In spite of his failure in this he remained on board. On the dreary, unbroken passage to Hobart Town, where provisions were to be taken on, relations between Dillon and Tytler became steadily worse. On a long and hazardous voyage there is no limit to the harm which a persistent trouble-maker may do; and Dillon, who had bent his whole will to the achievement of the task in hand, arrested Tytler for alleged incitement of the crew to mutiny and imprisoned him—for two hours. When they arrived at Hobart Town, Tytler, making himself out as the organizer of the expedition, obtained Dillon's conviction on a charge of assault. The judgment included a sentence of two months' imprisonment. It threatened the ruin of the expedition. But against one eventuality—the proposal of the Governor to send the ship to sea without him—Dillon was well prepared: his faithful friend, Buchert, whose services were indispensable, would serve no other commander; and the ship's papers had been sent off to Sydney. Friends of the captain eventually secured his release. Tytler and his supporters (including the first mate) then abandoned the expedition; and after the vacancies had been filled, Dillon sailed—first to Sydney, then to the Bay of Islands, then to Tongatapu, and from Tongatapu to Tikopia, which they reached early in September.

The goal was at last within reach. And now Buchert was able to bring on board a visitor from Vanikoro: he explained how the two lost ships had been cast ashore, how many of the men who were on them had been murdered, and how the survivors—protecting themselves behind a palisade on the seashore—had built a two-masted vessel in which they had at last put to sea again. So Vanikoro was not quite the end: but there could be little doubt that La Pérouse and his remaining followers had been engulfed by the ocean before they had gone far upon their long voyage back into known seas in the ill-sailing craft which they had built out of wreckage.

On the morning of 7 September the *Research* was in sight of Vanikoro; on the following day Buchert and a Tikopian established friendly relations with some of the natives; and on the 9th regular intercourse with the people began and continued for almost a month, until their departure on 7 October. The story they had learnt at Tikopia was confirmed and amplified by the Vanikorans, and its truth established by the many relics they managed to buy and from investigations ashore. There were the iron tiller of a large ship, domestic utensils, pieces of china, a silver vessel stamped with the fleur-de-lis, a large ship's bell decorated with religious symbols and stamped *"Bazin m'a fait"*, a small gun, and much else; and as each acticle was obtained the time and place of its purchase was carefully recorded and the record signed by Eugène Chaigneau, the French representative, and by the officers of the ship. Thus Dillon armed himself against sceptics as best he could. It was a great disappointment to find that one of the two survivors of whom he had heard was dead and that the other had left the island: but enough evidence had been collected to make identification of the wrecks quite certain.

When he returned to Sydney in December, Dillon was greeted with all the respect that was due to him. "He is an eccentric character," the *Sydney Gazette* wrote, "(he) has accomplished a most singular undertaking—and will meet with unprecedented applause." At the beginning of February the *Research* sailed for Calcutta, where she arrived on 7 April. In his absence, Dillon says, the company to which he had entrusted his affairs had become bankrupt and left him penniless: but the newspapers described his work; and from them his exploits were repeated by papers and reviews in Europe. In May Dillon sailed himself, as a passenger on the *Mary Ann*, for Europe, after an absence of twenty-two years. On 26 October he arrived at Plymouth. In November he travelled to France. Knowledge of his discoveries had, of course, long preceded him, and he was well received by the Minister of Marine. Three months later he was in Paris again. On 22 Feb. 1829, after almost exactly thirty-eight years, Charles X carried into effect the decree of 28 Feb. 1791: Dillon was granted the reward promised to the discoverer of the fate of La Pérouse—an indemnity of 10,000 francs for his personal expenses on the expedition and an annuity of 4,000 francs. On the same day he was created *Chevalier de l'Ordre royal de la Légion-d'Honneur*; and ten days later he was presented to the King.

From Paris, he returned to London to write his book, *Narrative and Successful Result of a Voyage in the South Seas, performed by order of the Government of British*

India, to ascertain the Actual Fate of La Pérouse's Expedition, interspersed with Accounts of the Religion, Manners, Customs, and Cannibal Practices of the South Sea Islanders.
It appeared in England towards the end of the year; and French and Dutch editions were published shortly afterwards. In the preface, he apologises for his defects as a writer. From one point of view, there is an element of truth in his disclaimer. The physical act of writing was still laborious for him—he employed the services of an amanuensis; and he had never learnt to spell. But his sensitiveness to language, his phenomenal memory, and his wide reading had made him a highly effective writer, in the broader sense.

Work on his book did not occupy all his time for long. Soon after the middle of the year he was back in Paris. The fame which he had already attained served but to increase his desire to be concerned in great events. In consultation with the Superior of the Irish College he developed a scheme for the establishment of Roman Catholic missions in the South Seas. He tied in with this a proposal for French commercial settlements in the Pacific, which was placed before the French government. The missionary side of the project, at any rate, obtained full approval. The government provided a naval storeship to take the missionaries to the islands, and in December Dillon, who was to accompany the expedition, was commissioned as French consul.

It was not long, however, before his personal leadership of the venture came under attack. His critics were primarily interested in replacing him by a candidate of their own. But, unfortunately, their arguments had some weight. Was there not a ring of insincerity about his championship of Catholicism and of France? Was he not a British subject? Had he not expressed admiration for Protestants like Samuel Marsden and John Williams? Was he not, indeed, a Freemason? All these things were true. But he fought back. It was in his power, he wrote, to gain for "Great France" "the finest provinces that ever the sun shone on". As to his religion, he told the Prince de Polignac: "I beg leave to observe that I am a Catholic, but not an enthusiast". Meanwhile the French government itself was heading for disaster; and the overthrow of the Bourbon monarchy in July 1830 finally killed Dillon's plans. Neither he nor his memoranda were forgotten in Paris, but his own chance of public office under the French was destroyed.

For four years he lingered in Europe, between London and Paris, seeking government office from the British, the French and the Belgians, attempting to promote schemes of settlement in the Pacific. In 1831 he seems to have aspired to an appointment connected with the proposed settlement of South Australia. In 1832 he published a pamphlet urging British colonisation in New Zealand. In May 1834 he wrote grandly to Eugène Chaigneau: "If I can be of any use to you here with the Prince de Talleyrand pray command me and I will instantly obey". But by that time he had arranged to return to the Pacific in a fairly humble commercial capacity. He had obtained financial support for a scheme to introduce machinery for the treatment of New Zealand flax.

He arrived back in Sydney in October 1834. "Among the arrivals by the *Prince Regent*", the *Sydney Gazette*

wrote, "we notice the name of captain—now the Chevalier Dillon—the celebrated navigator...." Roger Therry,
who met him at Government House, records that he
found him "like Yorick ... a fellow of infinite jest and
merriment". Then he proceeded to New Zealand, early
in 1835, and settled at Tauranga, with his flax machines.
These years were no less active than those which had
gone before. He remained at Tauranga only a year. Then,
he bought a small schooner, the *Jess*, and set out on the
last of his Pacific voyages, touching at a multitude of
islands between Tahiti and Fiji. All the old warmth flowed
back into his relations with his Polynesian friends: but,
in his dealings with Protestant missionaries, a new note
of irascibility had crept in. After he had landed stores for
Wesleyans at Vava'u, in Tonga, he wrote a scathing
letter to the missionary there telling him that, in the
the name of Christianity, he was using the money raised
by the English poor to oppress and corrupt the Tongans
and to live in luxury himself. And while he was convey-
ing other Wesleyans from Lakemba, in Lau, into the
centre of the Fiji group, thus making himself the agent
of another major missionary advance, he told Fijians on
board that his passengers were the exponents of a false
faith.

When he returned to Sydney, he prepared to sail
again for Europe. He was over 50 by now; and the life of
a trader was becoming too strenuous. His return to
London was a disillusioning experience. He was short of
money. His wife was ill. (She died in 1840 of "a decline".)
Worst of all, he was largely forgotten. He bombarded the
government with his views on the Pacific, attacked

Edward Gibbon Wakefield and the New Zealand Company with shrewdness and malicious wit, and sought unavailingly to obtain an official position. He tried to float a colonising venture of his own. He published a history of Russian expansion in Asia and issued a number of highly polemical pamphlets. One of the latter, about the missionaries in Tonga, so angered the Wesleyans that they had a book published with the title: *A Refutation of the Chevalier Dillon's Slanderous Attacks*. . . . He was still exuberant and flamboyant: but his years of adventure were over. He died in Paris on 9 Feb. 1847.

For many years, missionaries whom he had insulted continued to make unflattering references to him in their books and journals, and Polynesians who had been his friends proudly showed visitors gifts they had received from him. The map of the Pacific is bespattered with his name—Dillon's Rock, in Fiji (where he had defended himself and his companions in 1813), Dillon Bay (in Eromanga), Dillon's Anchorage (in Lakemba), and several names in Vanikoro. Yet, for all that, Peter Dillon was not a "great man" in the conventional sense. His quality lay in his personality, in the span of his interests. He belonged to the phase of Pacific history in which the establishment of trade and of Christian missions were the predominant motives for European activity. He stood aside from no aspect of the life of his times. But, through his interest in history and his agitation for intervention by the Powers, he also looked back to the age of exploration and forward to that of political imperialism.

Edna and Frank Bradlow

TREK AND COUNTER-TREK
IN SOUTH AFRICA[1]

The essence of South African history lies in the relationship between black and white. It is the story of the influx
and movement of peoples, of vain attempts to bolster up
frontiers by planting a white peasantry upon them, and
of equally unsuccessful efforts to lay down lines of cleav-
age and division. Above all, it is a story of the unack-
nowledged and almost subconscious need for contact
between black and white, whether in the waging of war
or in the search for trade.

Two main movements of population can be observed
in South Africa. The first, the European[2] influx, started
with Van Riebeeck's arrival in the Cape Peninsula in 1652
and gradually spread to the East and North; the second
was the southward movement of Bantu-speaking Africans.
Van Riebeeck brought with him the Dutch language and
a nucleus of Dutch and German settlers, with a sprinkling
of Swedes, who established the basic pattern for the future

[1] [Copyright © Edna and Frank Bradlow. Originally published in
History Today, IX (1959), pp. 326-35.]
[2] Henceforth used to denote "white".

Afrikaner nation in South Africa. The Bantu tribes were
migrants from the North. For many centuries Africa
south of the equator had been in a state of turbulence,
from which wave after wave of migrants had fled south-
wards. At the end of the eighteenth century, a few of
these tribes had reached the area of the Fish River in the
Eastern Cape, where they first came into touch with
Europeans. Behind them to the North, other migrant
tribes had halted, and the process of consolidation into
great Bantu nations was taking place. As tribes like the
Zulus attained their maximum military power, further
upheavals took place; and, by 1820, when the first British
settlers landed at Port Elizabeth, the turmoil was at its
height. These Southern tribes in their turn sent warring
off-shoots back into the North as far as Nyasaland: but,
from a South African point of view, their importance lies
in the relentless pressure that they exerted on the peoples
to the South, who were literally pushed into the arms of
the oncoming Europeans.

The indigenous population at the Cape on Van
Riebeeck's arrival were the inland Bushmen and the
coastal Hottentots—of little importance in South African
history except for the admixture of blood they gave to
the modern Cape Coloureds. They were classed together
as "natives" by the Dutch, and were more of a nuisance
than a danger. Van Riebeeck was the first of many legis-
lators who tried to carry out racial segregation, planting
a wild almond hedge to keep the Hottentots outside his
settlement. The Dutch East India Company, however,
urgently needed the Hottentots' cattle for victualling its
ships, and the Hottentots yearned for the tobacco and

trinkets of the European. The remains of the almond
hedge still stand, a monument of its ineffectiveness.
Already at this early stage, the seeds of many of the
country's future troubles were being sown. Van Riebeeck's
duty, as the servant of a trading company, was to provide
refreshments for passing ships, and nothing more. Colonisation was not the intention. It was only grudgingly that
the Company, finding itself short of provisions, allowed
nine free burghers to settle on small farms for the purpose
of growing corn and vegetables for revictualling ships,
and thereby established the European as a permanent

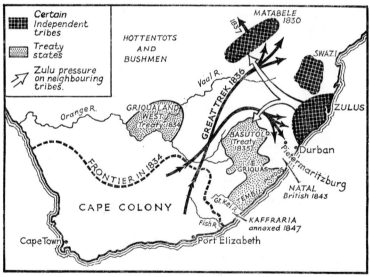

History Today map by S. H. Perrin based on A. M.
Healy and E. R. Vere-Hodge: *The Map Approach to
African History*, University Tutorial Press, 1959.

South Africa in the first half of the nineteenth century, showing the
Great Trek of the Boers and Zulu movements.

settler at the Cape. At the same time, the first slaves, of
Malay stock, were imported from the East to supplement
the labour supply. Their coming strengthened the belief
of the white settlers that manual work was for the black
man, and encouraged the Europeans "in their desire to
be well attended upon first before they will think of
serving others".[3]

Despite the Company's reluctance, the colonisation of
the Cape slowly continued. In 1688 the refugee Huguenots
arrived, a mere two hundred in number, but an ingredient
in the population so highly concentrated that it altered
and helped to fix the character of the young settlement.
It began to emerge now in the form of a colony, with a
settled agricultural population, independent of the trading
activities of the Dutch East India Company. Within two
generations, the Huguenots were absorbed by the Dutch
settlers. But they infused a certain refinement into the
rough "ocean tavern" atmosphere of their new home,
adding also a measure of their stern Calvinistic faith and
their own particular brand of sturdy independence.

By the beginning of the eighteenth century, the Cape
was already stretching far beyond the limits envisaged by
the Council of Seventeen, and the colonists were turning
their backs on the company and its restrictive legislation.
A class of frontiersman was evolving, the "trekboer" or
cattle farmer, who roamed the wooded kloofs with his
family, his waggon and his herds, endlessly searching for
water and pasturage, and shooting when the pot needed
provisions. These "trekboers" formed the vanguard of
South Africa's own internal white immigration. By 1702,

[3] Commissioner-General van Imhoff, on a visit to the Cape, in 1743.

the first contact had been made with the Bantu in the form of scattered Xhosa tribesmen in the East, and the pattern of future events began firmly to take shape.

The Bantu, of whom the Xhosas were a tribe, were semi-nomadic pastoralists, like the "trekboers", questing for water and grazing land in a country subject to searing droughts. In the story of population movements in South Africa, it was the similarities between the Bantu and the frontierman's modes of living that caused the interminable frontier clashes of the nineteenth century.

During the early nineteenth century, the Bantu on the Eastern Cape frontier were being harried in the rear by a vast movement of terror-stricken tribes known as the "mfecane", or crushing. So far as the historian can ever assign to any one agent the responsibility for such a confused, unorganised movement of people, the rise of the great Zulu king, Chaka, between 1818 and 1828 was of critical importance. His highly disciplined, beef-fed, celibate impis, with their new short stabbing spear, became the instrument of a gigantic policy of conquest, concentrated in Natal, but felt as far as Rhodesia in the North, and the Fish River in the South. Tribes that were not wiped out, or absorbed, fled before the terrible threat in their rear; in the North, great tracts of land were emptied, while the over-populated regions on the Eastern Cape frontier filled to bursting point.

In these circumstances, it was impossible to lay down a rigid boundary between black and white. Whether in fighting or bartering, the frontier as defined by a reluctant government was continually ignored, and the process of absorption through economic interdependence continued uninterrupted. From the time of Joachim Van Plettenberg (1774) onwards, Cape governors tried unavailingly to establish a frontier. The first of the frontier clashes between colonists and Xhosas, known as the Kaffir Wars, took place in 1779; by the time of the Second British Occupation in 1806, four had been fought.

The change in the Cape's government, which was a by-product of the Napoleonic wars, together with the arrival of 5,000 English settlers some fourteen years later, completely transformed the Cape. The colony emerged from its isolation to come within the political framework of a powerful empire, linked to a stable economic system. The way was now opened for the absorption of contemporary British ideas of humanitarianism and philanthropy. For these the evangelical centre, Exeter Hall, became a symbol in South Africa, both venerated and despised. The torch-bearers of the new ideas were the missionaries, often going too fast for the narrow, rigid, conservative community among whom they lived.

The arrival of the settlers in 1820 was part of the deliberate anglicising policy, in administration, law, and language, carried out by the Governor, Lord Charles Somerset, and the British Government during the early decades of the century. A fresh pattern in the white population began to emerge. Although brought out to occupy farming country on the Eastern frontier, and act as a buffer against the Bantu, most of the English settlers returned to, or established, the kind of milieu they knew best—the towns. For the next one hundred and twenty years this pattern persisted in South Africa—the Dutch remaining the rural population, the English the townspeople. These English settlers brought to a remote province some of the niceties of civilised behaviour. They established a newspaper, with "Fighting Bob" Godlonton as its vigorous, trenchant editor. And although many were ignorant and semi-literate, they posesssed a taste for independence, happily allied to a traditional English respect for government and the rule of law that was new on that restless frontier. True, the 1820 settlers were a small drop in the mighty ocean of emigration that flowed out of post-Napoleonic Britain, and whose main stream by-passed the Cape, going to Australia and America. But the mere counting of heads can in no way be equated with the impact these settlers made on life at the Cape.

Unfortunately, the sixth Kaffir War, in 1834, did much to destroy many of the practical effects that this settlement had on the Eastern frontier. The causes of this war lie buried deep in the ceaseless movements of the Southern Bantu, still experiencing the aftermath of the "mfecane". Inevitably, there were mutterings and complaints as land-hungry tribes swept across the border. Afterwards, for the white colonists, came "the cries of widows, the lamentations of the fatherless".

At the end of the war, the Governor, Sir Benjamin D'Urban, recommended the annexation of part of the grossly overpopulated "native territory" and its settlement by white colonists under British colonial law as a substitute for the ineffective rule of native chiefs. In London, the Aborigines Committee of the House of Commons was hearing evidence on the relations between British settlers and indigenous peoples in all parts of the Empire. Before D'Urban's plans for a new province were quite complete, the critical findings of this committee were published, and the Colonial Secretary, Lord Glenelg, vetoed the scheme.

The abandonment of this "Province of Queen Adelaide" and the start of the celebrated movement of the Cape Dutch population, known as the "Great Trek", occurred in the same year. Undoubtedly, dissatisfaction with the British government's handling of the Eastern frontier problems, and the consequent fear of insecurity, as expressed in Piet Retief's[4] Manifesto, sharpened existing discontent. But the Great Trek was primarily a speeding up of a natural process—the endless search for pasturage that, for over a century, had been the lot of the land-squandering "trekboer". The efforts of the British government to systematise land-holding only aggravated this organic need for more and more land. Close on the need for land came the need for labour, preferably cheap, in a country where the soil was hard and unyielding, and the climate pitiless. Measures like the 50th Ordinance, allowing Hottentots to move about the colony without passes, decreed by a government in the full flush of nineteenth-century humanitarianism, and the establishment of a Circuit Court open to both Hottentot and European, not only disturbed the Boer's traditional idea of the relationship between white masters and black servants, but also left him short of labour. Land, labour, and security were the three vital needs of the frontier farmer; and when they were denied he went elsewhere in search of them.

In the East, the Xhosas formed a solid black barrier

[4] Probably the most famous of the Trek leaders.

that the Boers could not penetrate. The natural flow of
the Trek was therefore to the North, towards what is
now the Transvaal, thence coming down the Drakens-
berg Mountains into present-day Natal. Owing to the
"mfecane", these lands were temporarily empty of their
indigenous inhabitants, other than the war-like Matabele
in the Transvaal and the Zulus in Natal. With the defeat
of these two powerful tribes, the Boers were able to
establish two republics, one across the Orange River,
eventually divided into the Transvaal and the Orange
Free State, and the other in Natal, annexed some years
later by the British.

The Trek opened up the interior of South Africa, and
at the same time posed the problem of how such distant
territories should be governed. The hinterland was now
sparsely, but almost exclusively, settled by the Dutch, who
had left the English colonists in possession of the growing
towns in coastal regions. Within twenty years, two Boer
Republics had been established and recognised by the
British government, and the process of "balkanisation"
in South Africa was well on its way.

Into the two republics, the Dutch "took the non-
literary and non-industrial habits of the eighteenth
century. Thus were fixed those attitudes and habits of
mind which later returned from exile profoundly to influence all South Africa."[5] Into the rolling lands north of
the Orange River, the Boers imported the old wasteful
farming methods, the right of every man and his sons to
own 6,000 acres each, and to use them as they wished.
And with them, too, went their strict Calvinistic beliefs,

[5] de Kiewiet: *A History of South Africa.*

their fierce conservatism, their belief that they were a "Chosen People" with a divinely appointed mission in South Africa, their determination to preserve "proper relations" between master and servant, black and white, based on a doctrine of no equality either in church or in state. In isolation, far away from even the faintest echo of the calls for freedom and liberty for the individual that were beginning to be heard in Europe and America, these attitudes fixed and hardened, and came to be regarded as a traditional way of life.

With an inconsistency frequent in South African history, this opening of the hinterland, instead of separating black and white, brought them into closer contact and rendered complete territorial segregation—as envisaged, for example, by the missionary Dr Philip—impractical and impossible for all time. The two streams of population now moved along the same path, one at a higher level than the other, one sluggishly, but always travelling in the same direction.

The white stream received little reinforcement from outside during the next thirty years. Compared with Australia and Canada, the amount of immigration was small and of no major importance; for South Africa, with its large native labour force, offered no inducement to a man who had no other capital than the strength of his arms. In 1857, two thousand German legionaries were settled on the Eastern frontier, and were followed in 1858 by 1,600 German civilians. They did little to change the existing pattern of the European population, most of them being absorbed into the English-speaking element by reason of the districts in which they settled. They, were

in fact, just another small addition to the already hetero-
geneous white population.

To successive Cape Governors, the Eastern frontier
continued to be a nightmare. Only a strange stroke of
fate—the mass cattle-killing carried out by the Xhosas,
encouraged by their unshakeable belief in witchcraft—
removed the ever-present threat of invasion under which
the colony had lived. Nonquase, the prophetess, had
promised them fat oxen and full cornbins and resurrection
of their dead warriors to drive the white man into the
sea. Instead, thousands of starving Xhosas, moved by
famine, streamed into the colony and, as cheap labourers,
became inextricably bound to its economy from this time
onward.

In distant Natal, at the same time, the need for cheap
labour introduced a further alien element of population
that was absorbed by neither of the two main streams.
For years, ivory had been the chief export of this colony
until sugar was introduced from Mauritius, bringing with
it, as an accessory, the immigrant Indian coolie. A scheme,
supervised by the government, had been started in 1860
for bringing in indentured labourers; and by 1865 over
six thousand coolies had arrived, aiding Natal on her way
to prosperity and adding to South Africa's multi-racial
problems. Meanwhile, the Natal Legislature looked no
farther ahead than the current year's sugar profits. Less
than thirty years later, this same Legislature was trying to
find ways of removing some of the colony's surplus
Indians, by passing discriminatory laws against them.

Not surprisingly, the Indian government refused to
allow indentured labourers to be signed on when the

Transvaal gold mines came into full production and labour was desperately needed. The anti-Indian laws in the Transvaal were even more discriminatory than those in Natal. A number of Indians, mostly traders and of a higher class than the untouchable coolie, had found their way into the Transvaal over the years. The Republic denied them all civil and political rights, forbade them to own fixed property and made them liable for registration—all of which was no more than an extension of the Republic's native policy. The Indians, at the time, had no political awareness. The main difficulty raised by their presence in the 1860s was that there were too few of them to supply all the labour that was needed. It was not until after the South African War that the Indian question, embarrassingly and acutely linked with the British government's problems in India, became an irritant in South African race relations.

It was the ever-present "native problem", within the general framework of South African conditions and affairs, that continued to be the source of all ills. Prospects in the 1860s were bleak. Wool had slumped; the opening of the Suez Canal was about to by-pass the "Tavern of the Seas"; overseas capital refused to be drawn into any more unremunerative investments. Drought followed drought; crops failed; and, inevitably, restless Africans began to press upon adjacent European lands. Behind much of the unrest was the hand of Moshweshwe, paramount chief of the Basuto, a man of high intelligence and diplomatic gifts, who coveted the rich cornlands of the Free State for his mountain people. But there were more organic causes for Bantu restiveness. It was the result of years of encroachment by the European farmer; of his use of land needed by his black opposite number; of over-population and underfeeding; and, always present, of a subconscious need—the need of the white man's ways.

This last need received a powerful stimulus from the discovery of diamonds near Kimberley in 1869. At a period when tribal authority was collapsing in every part of South Africa, the demand for labour on the diamond fields accelerated the process, destroying the African's accustomed way of life, and leaving him only one logical alternative. On the diamond fields, the Africans began to be industrialised. Here was completed the process that changed them into detribalised workers—a movement that for years had been proceeding more slowly in the rural areas, where an African dispossessed of his land by war came back to find a European farm, on which he thereafter lived as a squatter. The diamond fields were eventually annexed to the Cape Colony. But the liberal attitude to non-whites, then current at the Cape, was not applied to the workers on the diggings. There they were relegated to positions of inferiority and employed at low levels of skill, as was now to become customary all over South Africa.

At the same time, white immigration, which for years had been stagnant, swelled to a flood, although many of the newcomers were fortune-hunters rather than perman-ent settlers. With the immigrants came fresh capital, which financed the building of the railways, the extension of harbours and other public works. The impact of the indus-trial nineteenth century hit South Africa late, but none the less effectively. Hopes of federation between the two

English colonies and two republics began to be delicately expressed, in spite of obvious difficulties.

The fear of a large-scale African uprising was an ever-present consideration which underlay many of the Colonial Office's apparently inexplicable actions such as the inopportune annexation of the Transvaal in 1877. The threat really existed, as may readily be seen. Migratory labour at the diamond fields had opened up a large-scale traffic in guns, especially directed to that trouble spot, Basutoland. In the far North, the Transvaal Republic's authority had collapsed, and Dutch farmers were paying tribute to the Bantu chief Sekukuni. In Zululand, a new generation of warriors, led by Cetewayo, aspired to re-create the former glory of the Zulus by learning the uses of the illicit gun under strict military discipline. Their defeat of British troops at Isandhlwana was proof of the need for a strong, uniform native policy in all parts of South Africa. On the Eastern frontier, overpopulation and drought had set off an inevitable inter-tribal war, which spread into the colony. In 1878, the settlement of this conflict—the last Kaffir War—laid the basis for all future native territorial policy at the Cape. A large reserve, the Transkei, was established, unbroken by European farms, effectively administered and subject to a policy of secure land tenure and less wasteful methods of farming.

Federation under the British Crown might eventually have eased the racial difficulties, had some compromise been reached between the xenophobia of the Transvaal and the economic selfishness of the coastal colonies. So long as the Transvaal remained poverty-stricken and on the verge of collapse, federation even seemed possible.

But then, by one of those "economic windfalls" common to South African history, the richest gold-vein in the world was discovered on the Witwatersrand; the Transvaal became solvent and for the first time began to take the lead in South African affairs. At a moment "when political and racial separatism had become a creed with a large section of the Republican Boers ... the new forces of trade, capital and industry entered into their midst".[6] The discovery of gold led to the movement called by Marquard "the second Great Trek", which far outstripped the original in its intensity. Into a sparsely settled, close-knit rural community, moving along at the pace of the traditional ox-waggon, came a wide-awake, progressive, materialist motley, from all over Europe and America. The deep-level nature of the Rand gold deposits soon made it apparent that the gold mines were no transitory phenomenon, and that only big, highly mechanised companies could hope to mine the ore profitably. Unlike Kimberley, with its speculative individual diggers, the Rand was therefore occupied by settlers of a more stable character, who looked upon the Transvaal as their permanent home.

To this new, mainly English-speaking community, the Transvaal administration was frankly hostile. Little concession was made to the use of English in public affairs or schools; and, under the electoral laws of the Republic, these "Uitlanders"[7] were virtually disenfranchised. By 1895, the Uitlanders were outnumbering the Transvaal burghers by seven to three; and there was some sound

6 de Kiewiet: *A History of South Africa.*
7 i.e., "outlanders" or foreigners.

common sense in Kruger's declaration that "if we give them the franchise . . . we may as well give up the Republic". The Uitlanders brought the clamorous present into the unwilling orbit of a simple people, who had been content to let their rigorous racial exclusiveness and the ever-present Bible stand as twin bastions against the on-slaught of alien progress and absorption. Kruger is generally portrayed as an obstinately uncompromising opponent of the Uitlanders and their wishes. Considering his unfamiliarity with the problems of the fabulous Witwatersrand and its many bizarre inhabitants, intransigence was the only weapon left to him.

After 1895, when the full extent of the Rand mines became known, events moved swiftly. The Uitlanders began to importune most earnestly for their rights as citizens. Under the harsh Highveld sun, judgments were not always wise or mature; and, at the far-off Cape, the "Colossus" dreamed about and planned his uninterrupted red line from Cape to Cairo. The Jameson Raid and its repercussions form another chapter in a history of alternating compromise and intransigence, of "misinterpretations and the half knowledge by which contemporaries lived". Only after a bitterly fought war was the long-sought-after political confederation achieved, and that without achieving a truly unified white South African nation.

P. M. Holt

THE MAHDIA IN THE SUDAN[1]
1881-1898

I

Islam shares with Christianity a world-view in which
God is the Lord of History, and the story of humanity
is the realisation of a divine plan. In times of social and
political stress, Muslim communities have shown an
unusually heightened response to eschatological concepts
while individuals have seen themselves as actors in the
supreme crisis of the cosmic drama.

One such phenomenon, occurring in modern Islamic
history, was the Sudanese Mahdia of 1881 to 1898. This
movement produced events that aroused a particular and
painful interest in Egypt, of which in 1881 the Sudan was
a dependency, and in Britain. In English writings on the
Mahdia, the story is dominated by two alien figures,
Gordon and Kitchener; the events chronicled are mainly
hostilities in which British or British-officered forces
were involved, and the whole movement is seen as a foot-

---

[1] [Copyright © P. M. Holt. Originally published in *History Today*,
VIII (1958), pp. 187-95.]

note to imperial history, rather than a development of intrinsic interest. The circumstances of the Mahdi's rise to power have been described; but there has been little attempt to analyse the nature of his mission, or to set it in the context of Islamic and Sudanese history. The decade from the death of Gordon to the beginning of Kitchener's reconquest has been left in obscurity, although these were the years in which the Mahdi's successor, the Khalifa Abdallahi, exercised greater authority than any Sudanese before him—or any since until the establishment of the Republic of the Sudan in 1956.

One cause of this defective and episodic treatment lies in the limited range of the source-materials that until recently were alone available. British and Egyptian military records, the writings of soldiers and journalists, biographies and memoirs of European participants in the events formed the bulk of these. One solid history, based partly on Mahdist documents and oral evidence, lay out of the reach of most students in a single and rare Arabic edition. Authentic reports of conditions within the Sudan during the Mahdia were sparse, and excessive weight was given to the few and embittered accounts of European refugees, coloured on occasion to serve as war-propaganda in the years before the reconquest.

The clarification of the internal history of the Mahdist state, the analysis of the nature of the movement that created it, and the appreciation of the place of this period in Sudanese history, have now been facilitated by the archives which, after fifty years of obscurity, were brought to light by the Sudan Government shortly before the end of the Condominium. These Mahdist documents consist of perhaps 50,000 pieces, the overwhelming majority of them being manuscript Arabic records of the administration in the Sudan under the Mahdi and the Khalifa. They include a very large number of letters sent to the Khalifa by his provincial officials, giving almost a day-to-day picture of the situation for some districts and periods. The Khalifa's own letters are fewer, though still numerous, and the Mahdi's writings fewer still. The study of this enormous mass of material, which has attracted both Sudanese and foreign students, has made it clear that the old accounts of the Mahdia must be substantially revised; that it was an organised revolutionary movement, fostered by religious and economic causes, and resulting in the establishment of a territorial Islamic state. The nineteenth-century British view, that it was an outburst of fanaticism which produced a relapse into barbarism, is a crude over-simplification of a complex series of developments.

II

British writers on the Mahdia have tended to ascribe it to Egyptian oppression and mis-government. This is an inadequate explanation. The Egyptian administration was largely Ottoman in its outlook and personnel; its aims were to maintain or expand its frontiers, to preserve internal security and to collect the revenue; and, on the whole, it secured these aims by a mixture of *laissez-faire* and occasional repression. Contemporary Sudanese were by no means unanimously hostile to it, except at times when it interfered with their personal interests: but the nomads in particular resented all government and were unwilling taxpayers.

Egyptian historians are probably nearer to the mark when they indicate the attempt to suppress the slave-trade as a potent cause of the revolt. The most determined efforts at suppression were made by the reforming Khedive Ismail (1863-79); and its last phase was inaugurated when he concluded with Britain the Slave Trade Convention of 1877, which provided for the termination of slave-trading in the Sudan by 1889. Ismail's progressive humanitarianism was probably more damaging to his authority in the Sudan than all the faults of Egyptian rule since Muhammad Ali's conquest. Slavery was an institution permitted by Islam; hence the Khedive's acts were represented as irreligious, the result of his contacts with Christian Europe. Economically, the northern Sudan depended on slavery and the slave-trade. Furthermore, the implementation of a policy of suppression demanded endless time or, failing this, overwhelming force. Ismail had neither of these nor, towards the end of his reign, the financial resources necessary to back so radical a policy. His officials turned a blind eye to orders that they lacked power to enforce. Ismail therefore sought more reliable administrators outside the official cadre, which was composed largely of Turco-Egyptians. So began the recruitment of European and American officials, among whom the best known were Sir Samuel Baker and General Gordon.

These appointments were well-intentioned but unfortunate. The Europeans and Americans had as few resources at their disposal as their predecessors. Their

Paul Kruger. "Intransigence was the only weapon left to him."

Ox-waggons in Zululand.

Paul Popper

"No longer detached appendages of Empire but its participators and instruments." Curzon visits the Nizam.

Kitchener attending funeral of Prince Francis of Teck.

presence was an irritation to the Turco-Egyptian officials. They were Christians; and so their arrival gave substance to the popular belief that the Khedive was under the thumb of the infidels. They were incorruptible and conscientious, and thereby brought to the surface the antagonisms that their predecessors had allowed to sleep. On occasion they struck out blindly at their opponents, and won a temporary success at the cost of threatening the delicate balance of interests on which the Khedive's rule depended.

The revolt was assisted by developments in Eygpt. The deposition of Khedive Ismail in 1879, at the behest of the French and the British governments, made public the diminished powers of the Egyptian viceregal house. The installation of his son, Muhammad Tawfiq, as a puppet of the Dual Control; the Urabi revolt; and, a year after the Mahdia had begun, the British occupation of Egypt, were all indications of the growing weakness of Egypt. The Mahdia was organisationally independent of Urabi's movement and was unconcerned with Egyptian events: but there can be no doubt that they presented it with its opportunity to grow.

It would, however, be wrong to see in the Mahdia merely a revolt of disaffected slave-traders and others, taking advantage of a period of weakness to cast off the alien rule of Egypt. The material grievances of the northern Sudanese provided the movement with mass support; but the origin of the Mahdia was a demand for religious reform, its dominating emotion was religious, and it found its expression in the imagery of Islamic mysticism. This was a point that contemporary European writers found difficult to grasp; and the religious aspects of the Mahdia were usually derided as hypocrisy or denounced as fanaticism. Yet Islam has repeatedly given birth to militant reformist movements; and a series of these began in the eighteenth century. Two with a marked similarity to the Mahdia were the Wahhabi movement, originating in Najd, which, in alliance with the house of Saud, established its dominion over a large part of Arabia until its overthrow by Muhammad Ali Pasha in 1818, and the movement of Uthman dan Fodio (1754-1817), originally a religious teacher in what is now northern Nigeria.

These movements resembled the Mahdia in their aim, the restoration of Muslim society on what their founders believed to be the primitive Islamic model; their method, the *Jihad* or Holy War against unbelievers (meaning primarily Muslims who did not accept their tenets); and their result, the creation of a territorial Islamic state. But in two important respects they differed from the Sudanese movement. They took place at a time when traditional Muslim society was not yet directly threatened by the impact of Western Europe. It was the misfortune of the Mahdia to occur at the heyday of European imperialism in Africa, and in an area of critical importance to the imperialist powers. Hence its development was cut short, and its ideology, appearing against a background of nationalism and liberalism (which were already affecting Muslim thought), had a curiously archaic appearance.

The Mahdia differed also from the two earlier movements in that neither of their founders claimed the special status of a *mahdi*. This term implies a Muslim leader who receives unique guidance from God. The idea of a *mahdi*, developed early in Islam, was influenced by Christian beliefs of the Second Coming, and assumed numerous forms. Among the Sunni Muslims, which include those of the Sudan, Mahdism is a deposit of popular ideas and hopes, having particular emotional force in times of crisis, rather than a systematic and fully orthodox system of beliefs. The *mahdi*'s function is, in a traditional phrase, "to fill the earth with equity and justice, even as it has been filled with tyranny and oppression". The Sudanese Mahdi, in words he often used, regarded his mission as "the establishment of the Faith and the *Sunna*", i.e., the reputed custom of the Prophet, which serves as a source of law to guide his followers.

This, however, was no more than earlier Muslim reformers had sought to do. Why, then, did the Sudanese leader claim to be the Mahdi, thereby assuming a special and unique character for his mission? In so doing he was responding to a widespread popular feeling, that the time had come for the appearance of this divinely commissioned deliverer of Islam. One of his own letters describes how he himself had shared in this Mahdist hope and had at first expected the divine election to fall upon the leader of the Sanusi brotherhood, in what is now Libya. He was also legitimising his revolt against a Muslim ruler, the Khedive, by claiming a divine sanction. Finally, although the coming of the Mahdi was envisaged by theological systematisers as a unique event, heralding the Day of Judgment, the Muslim world has seen not a few *mahdis*. One of the most famous, Muhammad ibn Tumart

(c. 1078-c. 1130), arose on the western fringe of African Islam, with Berber tribal support, and created a force with which his successor founded the Almohad Empire in Morocco and Spain. A later crisis, the arrival of Bonaparte and the French in Egypt, produced another *mahdi*,

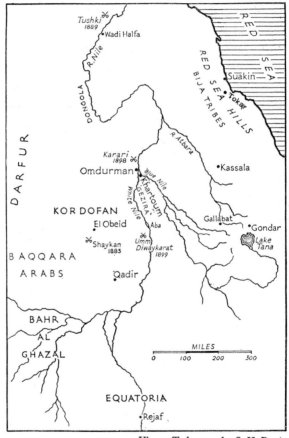

History Today map by S. H. Perrin

The Sudan

who stirred up Buhayra province, west of the Delta, to revolt, but was defeated by a French force. In assuming the title of *mahdi* at a time when Muslim rule in the Sudan and Egypt alike was feeling the pressure of Christendom, the Sudanese leader was conforming to a traditional pattern of Islamic reaction to crisis.

III

We have little detailed information about the career of Muhammad Ahmad ibn Abdallah before he manifested himself as the Mahdi on 29 June 1881. His family came from Dongola, a riverain province in the northern Sudan. He himself was about forty years old at the time of the manifestation, and already enjoyed a high repute for sanctity and asceticism. He had long been preaching a return to primitive Islam; and, although he had gained no distinguished adherents, he had many followers among the simpler folk, particularly in the districts around his retreat, the island of Aba in the White Nile, about 190 miles south of Khartoum. In the years immediately preceding the manifestation, he had travelled through Kordofan in the western Egyptian Sudan, and prepared the way for the outbreak of the revolt. Here was a wealthy Sudanese merchant-class, disgruntled at the attempts to suppress the slave trade. Here, too, and in Darfur further west and recently annexed, were the nomad Baqqara tribes, resentful of any government and willing supporters of a revolt that had a religious justification and that offered prospects of settling old scores and acquiring booty.

The manifestation in Aba was followed by the emigration to Qadir, a hill in southern Kordofan. The term used for this emigration (*Hijra*) and that given by the Mahdi to his followers (*Ansar*—not "dervishes", a term that he forbade to be used), were deliberately adopted from the usage of the Prophet. The *Ansar* defeated the Egyptian forces, which proved unexpectedly vulnerable, in a series of skirmishes and battles, while the Mahdi's agents harassed the administration in various parts of the Sudan in an elusive, guerilla warfare. The capture of the garrison towns was more difficult: but El Obeid, the provincial capital of Kordofan, fell on 19 Jan. 1883. Hopes of overthrowing the Mahdi were extinguished when an Egyptian expeditionary force, the pathetic remains of Urabi's troops under a British general, Hicks, was annihilated at Shaykan in Kordofan on 5 Nov. 1883. Egyptian authority in the west crumbled. Slatin, the Austrian-born governor of Darfur, and Lupton, the English governor of the Bahr al-Ghazal in the south, surrendered. Gordon was sent out on an ill-defined mission to the Sudan, his plans becoming more grandiose and fantastic as he went on. He was courageous, but lacking in cool judgment, and his influence with the Sudanese was infinitely less than the British public believed. Having brought himself into a situation where he could neither evacuate the Egyptian garrisons nor stay the Mahdi's advance, he died when Khartoum fell on 26 Jan. 1885.

When the Mahdi himself died, in his new capital of Omdurman on 22 Jun. 1885, he controlled most of the northern part of the former Egyptian Sudan. British and

Egyptian forces in Dongola province were soon to with-
draw to Wadi Halfa. The German-born governor of
Equatoria, Emin Pasha, maintained a tenuous authority
until he was "rescued" by H. M. Stanley's much publi-
cised expedition in 1889. The port of Suakin, which
never fell into Mahdist hands, formed a base for operations, ineffective until 1891, against Uthman Diqna
(Osman Digna), the military governor of the Red Sea
Hills, whose Beja followers, the Fuzzy-Wuzzies of
Kipling's verse, became part of the Victorian legend of
the Sudan. Yet in spite of his victories, the Mahdi died
with his mission unaccomplished. In a vision recounted
to the *Ansar* after the fall of El Obeid, he had foreseen the
conquest of the heart of the Muslim world. The vision
was not fulfilled; and the universal Mahdist state was
transformed during the next few years into a Muslim
monarchy over the northern Sudan.

IV

On the Mahdi's death, the supreme power was grasped
by his leading follower, the Khalifa Abdallahi ibn
Muhammad, who originated from the nomad Taaisha, a
tribe of Baqqara, i.e., cattle-owning Arabs of Darfur.
The Khalifa had exercised wide powers by delegation
from the Mahdi during the latter's lifetime: but his ac-
cession was unpopular with the relatives of the Mahdi
(the *Ashraf*) and the riverain Arabs (*Awlad al-balad*)
who formed the bulk of the ruling elite in the Mahdist
state and despised the uncouth Baqqara. This opposition
group had a young and inexperienced leader in the

Khalifa Muhammad Sharif, a kinsman of the Mahdi. They were in touch with the powerful military governor of Darfur, Muhammad Khalid, who began to march on Omdurman with his provincial forces. The Khalifa Abdallahi acted with promptitude and decision. A conspiracy of the *Ashraf* in Omdurman was forestalled. The troops in the capital were united under Abdallahi's brother, Yaqub; and Muhammad Sharif was required to affirm his loyalty to the regime. The army of Darfur was intercepted by Hamdan Abu Anja, an able general who was a client of Abdallahi. Muhammad Khalid was made a prisoner and his forces were taken over by Abu Anja. Meanwhile, the Khalifa Abdallahi was steadily increasing his grip on the administration by appointing his own kinsmen and clients to the military governorships and displacing the *Awlad al-balad* who had held them under the Mahdi.

Having surmounted this crisis, Abdallahi was able to resume the Mahdi's policy of the *Jihad* against unbelievers. Hostilities took place against tribes within the former Egyptian Sudan which were unwilling to accept Mahdist rule, and also against neighbouring territories. The Mahdist state had inherited an unsettled frontier with, and a tradition of warfare against, Abyssinia. From the frontier-town of Gallabat, Hamdan Abu Anja in 1888 raided as far as Gondar. After his death, an Abyssinian invasion of the Sudan was arrested on 9 Mar. 1889, by the battle of Gallabat in which the Abyssinian ruler, King John IV, was killed. The subsequent internal troubles of Abyssinia, until Menelik established his authority, ended large-scale hostilities.

In the western frontier-region of Darfur, the young military governor, Uthman Adam, suppressed a movement to re-establish the ancient sultanate, which had been extinguished when Darfur was annexed by Khedive Ismail in 1874. He was preparing hostilities against the independent neighbouring sultanates, when a rising under a messianic figure known as Abu Jummayza threatened for a time the whole Mahdist position in the west. The death of Abu Jummayza and the fortitude of Uthman Adam restored the situation: but the western expansion of Mahdism had ceased and, after Uthman Adam's death (1890), Darfur itself was precariously held. In the south, the *Ansar* failed to retain the Bahr al-Ghazal or to establish effective rule over the non-Arab tribes of the Upper Nile, although there were occasional raids, while a garrison and convict-station at Rejaf was linked with the capital by infrequent steamer-expeditions.

The critical frontier, however, was that with Egypt, against which the Mahdi had been planning a *Jihad* when he died. Operations here were entrusted to Abd al-Rahman al-Nujumi, a general belonging to the *Awlad al-balad*, from whom also the bulk of his forces were drawn. The suspicion has never died in the Sudan that Abdallahi deliberately sent al-Nujumi and his men on a hopeless quest, in order to destroy the strength of the opposition, but the lack of technical means to overcome the problems of transport and supply was the real cause of the expedition's failure. The campaign was calamitous. Famine dogged the expeditionary force throughout its advance from Dongola. The frontier-villages of Egypt failed to rally to the Mahdist cause. Al-Nujumi was killed and his

E.E.—H

army crushingly defeated at the battle of Tushki (Toski)
by Egyptian troops under Grenfell on 8 Aug. 1889.

V

The years 1889-90 were highly critical for the Khalifa
Abdallahi. The deaths of Abu Anja, al-Nujumi and
Uthman Adam removed three of his ablest generals.
Widespread famine was followed by devastating epi-
demics. The famine was made worse by the enforced
migration of the Taaisha and other Baqqara to Omdurman, where they formed a military support (of dubious
reliability) for the Khalifa and a burden upon the peasants
of the Gezira, the corn-growing peninsula between the
Blue and White Niles. The calling-in of the Baqqara
nomads temporarily strengthened the position of
Abdallahi, but deepened and made more permanent the
rift between himself and the *Awlad al-balad*, the most
sophisticated and competent of his subjects.

In these difficult circumstances the policy of the *Jihad*
was tacitly abandoned, although it remained a part of the
official ideology, and occasional bold raids across the
Egyptian frontier perturbed the War Offices of Cairo and
London. Trade was allowed to proceed with Upper Egypt
and Suakin. An elaborate fiscal system was developed,
handled by a bureaucracy using Egyptian methods and
largely staffed by former employees of the Egyptian
administration in the Sudan. Some attempts were made
at a reconciliation with the *Awlad al-balad*—Muhammad
Khalid was released from confinement and sent to govern
Dongola, where his presence symbolised Mahdist co-

existence with Egypt. But this phase ended with another
conspiracy of the *Ashraf* and *Awad al-balad* in Omdurman
(November 1891). For some days civil war threatened:
but the resources of the *Ashraf* were limited, while the
Khalifa wished to avoid hostilities in which the Baqqara
immigrants might slip from his control and loot Omdurman. The opposition was again politically outmanœuvred
and subsequently reduced piecemeal. The leaders were
exiled to Rejaf; and in March 1892 a council of notables
sentenced the Khalifa Muhammad Sharif to an igno-
minious imprisonment.

The five years which followed the revolt of the *Ashraf*
were characterised by a growing acceptance of Abdallahi's
rule throughout a diminished territory, by the tacit conversion of the Mahdist theocracy into a personal monarchy, and by growing European threats to the Mahdist
state. The failure of the revolt marked the end of serious
opposition. The Khalifa was now in effect (although
never in name) a Muslim sultan with his brother, Yaqub,
as his vizier. The sovereignty was to be hereditary,
Abdallahi's son, Uthman Shaykh al-Din, being his intended successor. The Khalifa's corps of orderlies was
transformed into a large standing army, the Bodyguard,
garrisoned near his residence. This quarter of Omdurman,
adjacent to the Mahdi's Tomb and the great open court-
yard of the Mosque, was cut off from the rest of the
teeming city by a wall that was several years in building.

Apart from a limited amount of trade, Abdallahi
discouraged contact with the neighbours of his state.
With Menelik of Abyssinia, who both before and after
Adowa proposed the establishment of peaceful relations,

he refused co-operation unless the Negus would totally exclude Europeans from his country. This attempt to maintain an iron curtain against Europe was already proving ineffective. Anglo-Egyptian forces from Suakin expelled Uthman Diqna from his base of Tokar in February 1891. The Italians, advancing from Eritrea, captured Kassala in July 1894. Thus in two important eastern sectors the Mahdist state was on the defensive. Belgian expeditions began from 1892 to penetrate into the districts of the Upper Nile and the Bahr al-Ghazal, and in 1894 clashed with Arabi Dafaallah, the military governor of Rejaf. From 1892 an advance through the Bahr al-Ghazal to the Nile became an objective of French policy, which was to materialise in the Marchand Expedition.

VI

The downfall of the Mahdist state resulted, not from its internal divisions, which under Abdallahi's strong rule it was outgrowing, but from the pressure of European imperialism. The diplomatic background of the Reconquest is a complicated story, in which the supposed interests of Egypt were not the important motive that contemporary publicity would suggest. The pretext for this first stage of the Reconquest was given by an Italian appeal for help after Adowa. The British military group in Egypt, headed in 1896 by Kitchener, had long been pressing Cromer and the British government for a forward policy and had won a first success in the Tokar campaign of 1891. British military and public opinion was still sensitive over the unsuccessful operations against the *Ansar* in the early years of the Mahdia. The cry of avenging Gordon, reflecting an outlook very different from Gordon's own, could be relied on to stimulate popular emotion.

Kitchener's successes rested on superior armaments and means of transport and supply. The military railway and the machine-gun enabled him to extend and supply his long lines of communication from his base at Wadi Halfa to the heart of the Mahdist state. His first campaign in 1896 ended Mahdist rule in Dongola. When the decision to continue the advance was taken, the riverain towns fell one by one. A large army under the command of Mahmud Ahmad, a lethargic and unintelligent warrior, was overwhelmed at the battle of the Atbara on Good Friday, 8 Apr. 1898. The Khalifa had still great reserves of men, and the Sudanese will to resist was unbroken, when Kitchener confronted him at Karari, a few miles north of Omdurman. In a hard-fought battle on 2 Sep. 1898, the flower of the *Ansar* fell before the machine-guns. Yaqub was among the slain, and Abdallahi himself was a fugitive when evening fell. For over twelve months, with a devoted remnant of his forces, he held out on the western bank of the White Nile, not far from the birth-place of the movement which had raised him to a throne. When the end came in the battle of Umm Diwaykarat on 24 Nov. 1899, his body was found lying upon the sheepskin that served him as a prayer-carpet, with his chief remaining followers at his side. His intended heir, Uthman Shaykh al-Din, was less fortunate. He was carried wounded from the field, to die a captive at Rosetta in the following year.

VII

Nineteenth-century British writings on the Mahdia give not so much a veracious picture of the movement as a reflexion of their authors' political preconceptions. A similar comment might be made on present-day popular Sudanese views about the Mahdia. The ideas that they reflect, however, are those of a later age and society—the nationalism and anti-colonialism of the modern Arab and African worlds. The Mahdi is seen as a national hero and a fighter against alien rule. But the religious side of his mission is not forgotten; and, although few perhaps would be prepared to concede him a unique status as Mahdi, he is revered as one in the succession of reformers and renewers of Islam

The Khalifa's reign and exploits are, by contrast, largely ignored. Abdallahi lived to see the downfall of the Mahdist state, whereas the Mahdi died at the height of his victorious career. The Khalifa's repression of the *Ashraf* and *Awlad al-balad* antagonised the most sophisticated class of his subjects, a class that regained its pre-eminence under the Condominium. His harsh centralisation displeased the anarchic nomads, who had shaken off the control of the Egyptian administration.

Nevertheless, by arresting the political disintegration of the northern Sudan, which was a likely consequence of the overthrow of Egyptian rule and the premature death of the Mahdi, the Khalifa Abdallahi contributed to the work that had been begun by the Funj kings of Sennar in the sixteenth century and continued by the soldiers and administrators of Muhammad Ali and Khedive Ismail.

With them and with his successors, the British and
Egyptian officials of the Condominium and the Sudanese
politicians of the last decade, he shares in the creation of
the modern Sudan.

Harold Blakemore

JOHN THOMAS NORTH,
THE NITRATE KING[1]

In the export of British capital and enterprise in the nineteenth and early twentieth centuries, the key role was
often played by individual *entrepreneurs* who created the
necessary interest among the investing public in the poten-
tiality of overseas resources and who made possible significant developments in the areas of their operations,
largely by the force of personal example. Such a man was
John Thomas North, 1842-96, known in his day as "The
Nitrate King", the principal promoter of an industry and
trade that was the economic prop of the Latin American
state of Chile from the 1880s until the First World War.
North was a remarkable Englishman who rose, in his own
words, "from mechanic to millionaire" in the space of
some twenty years, whose activities in the 1880s and 1890s
were a constant subject of interest to the commercial
press, and whose efforts to become a figure in society
were almost as dramatic as his manipulation of the nitrate
market on the London Stock Exchange. A self-made

[1] [Copyright © Harold Blakemore. Originally published in *History
Today*, XII (1962), 467-75.]

entrepreneur, endowed with considerable business acumen and an ebullient character, North belongs to the age of Cecil Rhodes and Barney Barnato, though, unlike them, he is almost completely unremembered in his own country. But he has a permanent place in the history of Chile and in the history of British commercial relations with Latin America.

The decades that witnessed North's rise to prominence and the growth of the British nitrate industry in Chile were years of economic development for many countries in Latin America, development that was to a large extent fertilised by British capital. By 1880, some £123,000,000 was invested in government loans and over £50,000,000 in productive enterprises such as railways, docks, telegraphs, and mines: by 1890, however, these figures had risen to £193,000,000 and £230,000,000 respectively, and represented the keen interest shown by British investors in the continent with which, throughout the nineteenth century, the United Kingdom had very close ties of commerce and sentiment alike.

The bulk of British capital invested in Latin America was directed to Argentina, Brazil, Chile, Uruguay, and Mexico, and, among these, Chile had long enjoyed a reputation for political calm and orderly government. Of the foreign commercial communities in Chile, the British predominated: by 1820, at least twelve firms had been established in Valparaiso, the dominant trading centre and port of the republic, and forty years later almost two thousand British subjects—half the total for the whole country—were domiciled there. Later in the century, indeed, one envious American writer went so far as to say that Valparaiso, with almost its entire trade controlled by Englishmen, its transactions conducted in pounds sterling, its English newspaper, *The Chilean Times*, and the virtually exclusive use of the English language, was "nothing more than an English colony". Between England and Chile there were particular affinities that had their origin in the period when Chile was fighting for her independence from Spain: Chileans long remembered Canning's role in the diplomacy of that period and Lord Cochrane's command of their navy; they sent their midshipmen to train on British vessels throughout the nineteenth century, and the history of the republic was studded with British names such as Edwards, Ross, and Blest, representatives of the great Anglo-Chilean families deriving from the early years of the century. British esteem for Chile grew as, like Brazil, she remained an oasis of calm in a turbulent continent.

Chile's reputation was enhanced by her defeat of Bolivia and Peru in the War of the Pacific, 1879-82, fought largely to determine the ownership of the rich nitrate provinces of Tarapacá and Antofagasta, the former Peruvian, the latter Bolivian. Nitrate was not important until the 1870s: before then, it was guano, the manure of untold millions of seabirds, that brought Peru the bulk of her revenue between 1840 and 1870. Guano was in great demand in Europe and America as an efficient natural fertiliser, rich in nitrogen: but, when the major Peruvian deposits on the Chincha Isles began to peter out in the 1860s, the British and other concerns active in the guano trade turned their attention to the natural nitrate of Tarapacá and Antofagasta, the major sources of this valuable fertiliser. At first, the Peruvian and Bolivian governments simply levied an export tax on nitrate shipments, leaving the ownership of the nitrate works or *oficinas* in private hands, mainly British and Chilean. In 1873, however, the Peruvian government, then on the verge of bankruptcy, raised the duty on nitrate and, two years later, passed laws that threw the whole industry into confusion. In May 1875, the Peruvian Executive was authorised to raise a loan of £7,000,000, of which £4,000,000 was to be used to buy out the foreign owners of *oficinas* who were to receive bonds made payable to bearer, carrying an annual interest of eight per cent and redeemable within two years by the government. This attempt to nationalise the nitrate industry produced nothing but uncertainty and depression in the nitrate market: the bonds were issued, but Peru failed to raise the loan to redeem them, and the position deteriorated further when war broke out in 1879 between Chile on the one hand and Bolivia and Peru on the other. The origins of the war were many and involved, but the results were clear and definite: Chile, victorious on land and sea, compelled her adversaries to sue for peace, taking as spoils of war the nitrate provinces of Tarapacá and Antofagasta.

During the war, great uncertainty prevailed among the holders of Peruvian nitrate bonds, in effect the title-deeds to the *oficinas*, as they did not know what would happen to their certificates in the event of a Chilean victory. Already before the war, owing to the policies of the Peruvian government, nitrate bonds were selling in Lima at sixty per cent of their nominal value, but by 1881 certificates originally worth £180 were selling at £20 to £30 only. In these circumstances, speculators, counting on a Chilean victory and, possibly with inside information, on the Chilean government's subsequent return of the *oficinas* to private hands, bought up large quantities of the depreciated bonds. Chief among these speculators was the man whose name later became synonymous with nitrate on the London Stock Exchange, John Thomas North.

At that time, North was already well known on the Pacific coast of South America. Born near Leeds, Yorkshire, in 1842, the son of a coal merchant, he first went to Peru in 1869 when the engineering firm of Fowler & Company, his employers since 1863, sent him out to set up machinery for the extraction of nitrate. He left their service in 1871 to manage an *oficina* near the principal port of Tarapacá, Iquique, and, within four years, he had acquired sufficient capital to purchase his own nitrate works. Other opportunities for advancement soon presented themselves. Water was scarce in the desert regions where nitrate was extracted; accordingly, in 1878, the Tarapacá Water Company was founded at Iquique to bring water by tanker from Arica. North promptly rented the Company's tankers for two years, adding to them an old vessel of his own, but, when Chilean forces overran Tarapacá early in the war with Peru, he secured recognition from the Chilean government as sole owner of the business, the Company's owners having fled the province. Although the property suffered damage during the war, North obtained partial compensation for this from the Chilean government afterwards and soon established a monopoly for the supply of water to the nitrate areas.

But the War of the Pacific did much more than this for the rising young *entrepreneur*; it presented him with a splendid opportunity of securing a dominant position in the nitrate industry itself. North went to Peru when that country was in chaos and the owners of nitrate bonds were hastily disposing of their holdings for whatever price they could get for them. In Lima, he bought up as many bonds as he could lay his hands on, and it is not unlikely that he knew the Chilean government intended to recognise the certificates as the title-deeds to the nitrate fields, for he was assisted in his activities by a certain Robert Harvey, like North, an engineer by training. Harvey had been Inspector-General of Nitrate to the Peruvian government and became a leading counsellor to the Chilean government in nitrate matters when their troops occupied Tarapacá: he may well have been an important factor in the Chilean government's decision to return the industry to private ownership, a decision announced by a series of decrees in 1881-2. Another English expatriate, John Dawson, played an essential role in these operations: as head of the Iquique branch of the Bank of Valparaiso, it was he who advanced North and Harvey the funds for buying the nitrate bonds. At the end of the war, therefore, this enterprising trio found themselves the virtual owners of the cream of the nitrate fields, worth much more than they had paid for them. The bonds of one *oficina*, that of Ramirez for example, cost Harvey £5,000, one-third of their real value: the property was sold to the Liverpool Nitrate Company on its formation in 1883 for £50,000, the Company itself being capitalised at more than double this figure.

North returned to England in 1882 to effect the second stage of the enterprise, the floating of companies to engage in nitrate extraction and trade. Between that date and his death, in 1896, he was connected, at one time or another, with more than two-thirds of the British joint-stock companies involved. He and his associates founded the Liverpool Nitrate Company in 1883, the Colorado Nitrate Company in 1885 and the Primitiva Nitrate Company in 1886, North himself being Chairman of the Board of all three by 1888. He was a born promoter with a remarkable gift for gaining people's confidence with his bluff and optimistic manner. In the mid 1880s, with nitrate in great demand in Europe, all went well and dividends were high: the Liverpool Company paid twenty-six per cent in 1885, twenty per cent in 1886, and forty per cent in both 1887 and 1888 on its £25 shares, while both the Colorado and Primitiva Companies paid dividends of from ten to fifteen per cent in these years. Other nitrate properties in Chile had still to be turned into companies and, with the earlier ones paying such high dividends, nitrate shares were in great demand when a number of new companies were floated during 1888 and 1889. By now, North had his enemies who were beginning to wonder when the process would end and how soon the nitrate market would collapse under the weight of so many concerns. *The Economist* was dubious from the start about North: on 7 Jul. 1888, it wondered sceptically "how far the securities of these undertakings (the new companies) are held by the public, for, although industriously puffed, there is reason to believe they are still largely in the hands of the promoters, who are seeking to work them off upon investors". The promoters were not disturbed and neither were the subscribers, only too anxious to seek a share in the great fortunes made by the nitrate capitalists and captivated by North's shining example.

North's projection of a public image to inspire confidence in his promotions was the key factor in his success. Part of this was North the successful businessman who had created a new network of economic interests. He was the centre of the "nitrate circle"; indeed he soon acquired the sobriquet "The Nitrate King", and appropriate homage was paid to him. "Put North's name on a costermonger's cart," said *The Financial News* in May 1888, "turn it into a limited liability company, and the shares will be selling at 300 per cent premium before they are an hour old ... North is a Pactolus among promoters. Whatever he touches turns, if not to gold, at least to premiums." And his empire continued to grow: his water monopoly in Tarapacá became the basis of the Tarapacá Waterworks Company, founded in 1888, with a capital of £400,000; the same year saw the foundation of the Bank of Tarapacá and London, with none other than John Dawson as manager at Iquique; a year later, North and Harvey founded the Nitrates Provisions Supply Company, and, perhaps most important, in 1888 North secured a powerful holding in the Nitrate Railways Company, which operated the only railway in Tarapacá.

Building up his business reputation and fortune was one way for North to impress the world; another was to cut a figure in society. Like many men of humble origin who attain to positions of wealth and influence, North sought to dazzle with ostentation. At vast expense, he built at Avery Hill, Eltham, Kent, an ornate mansion in spacious parkland. The building, Italianate in style, was surmounted by a large cupola, visible for miles around, and the timber used in the construction was specially shipped from South America. At the entrance to the main hall stood two large gates of decorative ironwork, reputedly seized from the Cathedral of Lima by Chilean troops in the War of the Pacific, and outside, in addition to gardens, orchards, stables, and kennels, there was a further reminder of the scenes of North's early labours, a large conservatory of glass and iron in which his guests might see a picture of South American flora in the heart of Kent. Avery Hill became the social centre of the new nitrate society and its owner an important figure in the life of his adopted county. Master of the West Kent Hunt, Honorary Colonel of the Regiment of Volunteers of Tower Hamlets, which he equipped out of his own pocket, friend of Lords Dorchester and Randolph Churchill, North spared no effort and no expense to realise a social ambition commensurate with his commercial success. Part of his popularity with the general public sprang from his sporting interests: he established a reputation as a bloodstock owner and breeder of greyhounds; one of his dogs won the Waterloo Cup three times. W. G. Grace, of Gloucestershire and England, dedicated his book *The History of a Hundred Centuries* to North, who was also known for his patronage of the boxing ring.

Accounts of North's benevolence were legion, and, in

particular, he was a benefactor of his birthplace. In 1888, when destruction threatened the old abbey of Kirkstall, near Leeds, he paid £10,000 for the building and gave it to the city, as well as £5,000 to the Leeds Infirmary and other sums for charitable and civic purposes. For these services to his native city, and in recognition of his other achievements, he was installed on 26 Jan. 1889, as the first Honorary Freeman of Leeds.

City Art Gallery, Leeds.

Colonel North as a sportsman. Drawing by Phil May.

E.E.—I

Thus, in business and in society, "the Nitrate King" prospered, despite the warnings of such critics as *The Economist*, which consistently accused North of covering up unpleasant truths about the future prospects of nitrate with displays of ostentatious *bonhomie*. The paper was concerned about the state of the nitrate market which, by the end of 1888, was entering a period of instability, owing to growing disequilibrium between supply and demand. This had happened before: a saturated market in the early 1880s led the leading companies to form a combination to restrict output until stocks were reduced and prices in Europe rose, and by 1886 there was a marked recovery for sales and, therefore, dividends for the companies. The chief market for nitrates was continental Europe, and, in particular, the sugar-beet agriculture of Germany and France: in 1887, growers there took over 245,000 tons, compared with 56,000 tons imported into Great Britain and 30,000 tons into the United States. But the recovery in nitrates was now being jeopardised by the formation of new companies in which North had a leading hand, and the new investors, not unnaturally in view of his scintillating rise to fame and fortune, expected high dividends: the temptation to produce at full capacity was, therefore, great, despite the deteriorating condition of the world market. Thus, the circumstances surrounding the formation of the first restrictive combination, which had collapsed in 1886, were about to be repeated.

But the times had changed. The Chilean government now derived almost half its revenue from the export duty on nitrate, and, under its able President, José Manuel Balmaceda, was spending large sums on impressive public works. It could not view with equanimity the possible curtailment of its revenue as the result of unilateral action by the foreign nitrate capitalists. Balmaceda began to give vague hints in public speeches that the government might be obliged to look again at the *laissez-faire* policy it had hitherto followed with regard to nitrates, and conflict between the foreign owners of the works and the Chilean government was confidently predicted by the commercial press. One of North's concerns in Chile had already come under attack, the Nitrate Railways Company, linking the ports of Iquique and Pisagua with the nitrate grounds. This railway was built in the 1870s by virtue of an exclusive concession from the Peruvian government whereby no other line might be built in Tarapacá for twenty-five years, but its history from the time that Chile took over the province was one long legal wrangle between the government and the Company. The latter, holding a quasi-monopoly on transport in Tarapacá, levied a high freight charge on nitrate shipments, and was under constant pressure from both the government and nitrate producers outside the North circle to reduce it. The government sought to show in the Chilean courts that the original concession was invalid and their battle with the Company came to a head in 1889 when the Council of State, the highest judicial authority, ruled that the Executive Power was competent to adjudicate the issue. As the latter was President Balmaceda there was no doubt of the result.

With nitrates in the doldrums, uncertainty in the air about the Chilean government's intentions, and investors worried, it was time for North to take a hand by visiting

Chile to see for himself what was happening. The visit began impressively with a "farewell" ball at the Hotel Metropole on 4 Jan. 1889, when a thousand guests representing what *The South American Journal* called the "aristocracy, the plutocracy and histrionocracy of the kingdom" enjoyed North's lavish hospitality; it cost him £10,000. He left Liverpool on 6 February, with his wife, his secretary, Melton R. Prior, staff artist of *The Illustrated London News*, himself a director of the Nitrate Railways Company, Montagu Vizetelly of *The Financial Times*, and, surprising to some, William Howard Russell, doyen of correspondents, who was accompanied by his wife. It was alleged at the time that Russell was induced by an honorarium of £15,000 to go and write a favourable report on North's interests, though, in fact, Russell only agreed to go if he could state his own opinions, which he did subsequently in his book, *A Visit to Chile and the Nitrate Fields of Tarapacá*.

Arriving at Coronel in southern Chile on 16 Mar. 1889, the party proceeded northwards on what was more of a royal progress than a simple visit. North gave a series of banquets that focused the country's attention on "*Coronel Juan del Norte, el rey de salitre*", and which gave "the Nitrate King" excellent opportunities to display his natural gift of showmanship. He dined the Chilean press, met civic dignitaries, indulged his philanthropic reputation and gratified the public by presenting two thoroughbred sires to the State Agricultural Experimental Station.

Meanwhile, President Balmaceda had recently returned from a tour of the nitrate regions where, in March, he had again referred to the dangers of foreign monopoly control and had strongly hinted that the Nitrate Railways' concession would soon come to an end. That the shrewd statesman and the forceful *entrepreneur* should meet was, perhaps, inevitable, and they did so on three occasions in March and April 1889. Russell, who was present, wrote later that the English party was cordially received by Balmaceda who intimated that "he had not the smallest intention of making war on vested interests", though he told North bluntly that he was offering too low a price for a new nitrate field he wished to buy. How far North was satisfied, it is impossible to say: the President was a clever man whose affability often concealed his true thoughts, and it probably suited his purpose to give vague verbal assurances, still leaving room for doubt in North's mind, so that the latter might think twice before embarking on actions likely to antagonise the government such as a new combination to restrict output of nitrate.

If North had met his match, at last, he was clever enough to conceal his doubts, and went on his socially triumphal way, calling at Iquique, New York, Paris, and Brussels on his way home in July. What he meant to nitrate shares was indicated by *The Economist* on 3 Aug. 1889:

> When the "Nitrate King" went to Chile [the paper said], the market lost its buoyancy . . . prices fell away rapidly and . . . continued to decline, until it was announced that the leader of the market was on the point of returning . . . but it was not until Colonel North had actually reached our shores that anything like strength was restored to the market.

But as 1890 came, and the long-predicted and more permanent recovery did not materialise, North had to work hard to retain the investors' confidence. He dominated his companies, issued reassuring statements, offered to buy out the worried—which usually persuaded them not to sell—and by bluff and guile preserved his reputation. At the same time, he carefully unloaded his holdings in those companies for which the writing was on the wall: in 1888 he had held 16,000 shares in the Nitrate Railways Company, but by 1896 he had less than 400.

Events in Chile then came to his rescue. Any threats there that might have been posed by President Balmaceda —though that is a moot point—were removed during 1891. In that year, a long-maturing conflict between the President and his Congress over their powers under the constitution exploded into civil war which lasted for eight months and was one of the strangest wars in modern history. Congress, supported by the navy, seized the nitrate areas to obtain the duty on shipments, but could not attack Balmaceda, who held the rest of the country, since they lacked arms. Balmaceda, supported by the army, could not attack the Congress as he had no fleet and the barren Atacama desert lay between them. An eight-months' stalemate between "the whale and the elephant", as the British Minister to Chile described the antagonists, was only ended in August 1891, when the Congressionalist forces, having secured arms from abroad before Balmaceda obtained his ships, landed in central Chile and defeated his troops in battle. Balmaceda committed suicide.

During the war, nitrate producers took advantage of the Chilean government's preoccupations to form the second restrictive combine and use up stocks of the fertiliser. Production was also curtailed by wartime dislocation as workers in the nitrate fields made up the Congressional army. Prices and share quotations both rose in 1891 and North was back in favour, particularly after August, since he was believed to have friendly relations with the victorious new government in Chile. This partly arose from the fact that during the war the Balmacedist press had frequently alleged that the real cause of the war was an unholy alliance of Chilean landed and banking interests with foreign nitrate capitalists, all of whom feared Balmaceda, and Congress was, in fact, the preserve of these Chilean interests. This theme found support at the time with the American Minister in Chile, Patrick Egan, one-time Treasurer of the Irish Land League, who was virulently anti-British, and also with one Maurice Hervey, sent out specially by *The Times* to report on the war. Hervey sent home sensational despatches, sometimes pointedly, though not explicitly, referring to North. Thus, on 19 May 1891, *The Times* printed his statement that "without quoting names, some of which are as well known upon the London Stock Exchange as the cardinal points of the compass ... the instigators, the wire-pullers, the financial supporters of the so-called revolution were, and are, the English or Anglo-Chilean owners of the vast nitrate deposits in Tarapacá", an allegation repeated later, again without proof, in his book *Dark Days in Chile*. Hervey was recalled in May to substantiate such charges and because his reports on Chile were so much at variance with all other sources of information, there was some suggestion that he had been bribed by Balmacedists.

Hervey could not provide *The Times* with the required proof and he disappeared from the scene shortly after his return to London, but his book and the Balmacedist propaganda against foreign nitrate interests have been the source of much speculation by historians, particularly as the revolution of 1891 was a turning-point in the history of Chile.

Clearly, if North and others had helped to suborn revolution in Chile, evidence would be very hard to find, and, indeed, there is none that is not vitiated by its source. It is perhaps significant that in the Political Testament that President Balmaceda wrote before committing suicide, in which he dilated on the causes and possible consequences of the revolution, there is not one word about economic interests. And, though it is also a negative point, the new government in Chile, far from being friendly towards foreign nitrate interests, not only carried through Balmaceda's policy on the Nitrate Railways Company, but also encouraged Chileans to buy nitrate grounds in 1892 and 1893 to weaken the foreign monopoly.

By 1894, interest in nitrates had declined among English investors. The second combination collapsed in that year, there was a fall in confidence in the Chilean government, and production was again outstripping demand. Moreover, it was beginning to be appreciated that North and his friends had not been exactly honest with shareholders. But he bluffed to the end: as late as November 1895, at a meeting called to discuss the winding-up and reorganisation of the Primitiva Company, North could still paint a rosy picture, pointing out that he still held 5,000 shares. He did not mention that he had unloaded twice that number in the previous five years. In fact, he had long since cushioned himself against the end of the nitrate boom by investing in collieries in England, factories in Paris and St Etienne, cement works in Brussels, tramways in Egypt and gold-mines in Australia. Not until after his death was it realised how overcapitalised were his companies and how much trading in securities had gone on; large numbers of investors gave him their confidence throughout, so powerful was the force of his personality. And he continued to play his public role: in 1895 he stood as Parliamentary candidate at West Leeds for the Conservatives against Herbert Gladstone, and though he lost by ninety-six votes after a recount, he provided the constituents with a spectacular campaign. Eschewing political speeches, he promised government contracts for local industries if he were elected, offered advice to racing enthusiasts, and distributed handkerchiefs engraved with his portrait, all the while riding on a fire-engine with well-known pugilists.

North died of a heart attack on 5 May 1896, while taking the chair at a board meeting of the Buena Ventura Nitrate Company in Gracechurch Street. His funeral at Eltham, which went into mourning, was attended by huge crowds from all walks of life, and the telegraph office in the town was so flooded by messages of condolence to the family that it had to increase its staff and remain open at night from 6 to 9 May. Letters of sympathy came from the Prince of Wales, the Khedive of Egypt, and the King of the Belgians, who also sent a representative to the funeral.

North's obituary notices reflected the attitudes that the

journals had taken to him during his lifetime. To his strongest critic, *The Economist*, he was "from first to last just a workman who had made a great fortune . . . and loved to proclaim it by extravagant expenditure and ostentatious display. . . . His great notion of hospitality was to drown his friends in champagne." But the paper also recognised his inherent ability, boldness, and personality. *The South American Journal* was more charitable to North, as, indeed, it had been throughout: "though not a man of much culture or high educational attainments", it said, "he was eminently gifted with qualities of judgement, prevision and promptitude which lead the way to conspicuous success in business enterprise or speculation". But whatever his methods, and they were sometimes less than honest, John Thomas North was a remarkable self-made man who began life as a penniless engineer and died almost a millionaire, and he deserves to be remembered in the country of his origin as he is in that South American republic on the other side of the world with which Britain has had such close links for so long.

Michael Edwardes

THE VICEROYALTY OF
LORD CURZON[1]

> To me the message is carved in granite, it is hewn out
> of the rock of doom—that our work is righteous
> and that it shall endure.

To those who listened in London's Mansion House on a
July day in 1904, these words spoken by a Viceroy of
India could only have confirmed their deepest beliefs in
Britain's imperial mission. The speaker, who had just
received the Freedom of the City, was George Nathaniel
Curzon, who seemed to embody with his masterful
energy and incisive brilliance of mind the "vitality of an
unexhausted purpose", Britain's purpose in her vast Asian
possessions. No doubts assailed Lord Curzon, no pessi-
mism was allowed to fray the edges of his imperial vision,
not even the hymn "Onward Christian Soldiers", rejected by Curzon himself from the programme of the
great Durbar held in Delhi the year before because it
contained the lines "Crowns and Thrones may perish,
Kingdoms rise and wane". Yet now, as we look back upon

[1] [Copyright © Michael Edwardes. Originally published in *History
Today*, XII (1962), pp. 833-44.]

the British Indian empire, we can see that instead of being the founder of a new period of imperial activity, he was the usher of one of slow disintegration. His Viceroyalty was to lead not to a restatement of power but to a failure of strength and purpose.

The two great Governors-General of modern British India, Dalhousie and Curzon, had much in common. Both were impatient for change, both had an arrogant faith in their own judgment above all others', and both have left lasting legacies to the independent India that neither really believed would ever come about. Modern Indians have come to accept Dalhousie as one of the great men of their *own* history. Curzon, perhaps because he is still within the net of living memory, continues to await acceptance.

The appointment of Viceroy, the most important office next to Prime Minister under the British Crown, was too often made without much reference to the suitability of the candidate.   The choice of Curzon, at least upon the surface, could not have been more apposite. He was young, only thirty-nine, when his appointment was announced in August 1898. Only Dalhousie, at thirty-six, had been younger. Apart from Lord Lawrence, who had been an active administrator in India before becoming Viceroy in 1864, he was the only Viceroy who had personal knowledge of India before taking up office. It had always been his dream one day to govern India, and he had single-mindedly prepared himself for the task. On a visit in 1887, he had looked at the gates of Government House in Calcutta, a mansion that by coincidence had been copied from his father's ancestral home, Kedleston Hall in Derbyshire, and said: "The next time I enter those gates it shall be as Viceroy". Eleven years later his prophecy was fulfilled.

The idea of India, of "an empire more populous, more beneficent and more amazing than that of Rome", had taken a grip of him; and yet Curzon's vision was not a romantic daydream. He went about, travelling throughout Asia, learning, as he put it, at the "University in which the scholar never takes a degree". He visited all the countries of the East and made a journey through Russian Central Asia. He wrote and published books on his experiences. He believed—and quite rightly—that India was "the political pillar of the Asiatic continent". When, in 1891, he was appointed Under-Secretary of State for India, he probably knew more about Asia than anyone else in the government. He was, however, only to hold office until the following year, when the Conservatives were defeated at the polls and Mr Gladstone and the Liberals took office.

Curzon set off on his travels again. His researches confirmed his belief that India was the "true fulcrum of Asiatic dominion" and furthermore that "the secret of the mastery of the world" was "if only they knew it, in the possession of the British people". By 1895, when the Conservatives had returned to power, Curzon felt he was ready to tackle the problems of Britain's Indian empire. But before the opportunity came he was to spend three years in the House of Commons as Under-Secretary for Foreign Affairs. It was this man, unshakeably convinced not only of his own mission but also of Britain's, which he believed the same, who was to be sent out to govern

Lord Curzon as Under-Secretary of State, conducting
Parliamentary business. Caricature by Harry Furniss.

and revitalise India. Curzon was admirably suited to "take up the White Man's burden", to obey the call of duty and to administer an empire in the finest tradition of imperial responsibility. Power, duty, and efficiency were the watchwords of imperialism, and nothing petty would be allowed to interfere with its civilising mission. Curzon's Viceroyalty was to be the last expression of the cold morality of the Utilitarians. "If I were asked," said Curzon, defining his creed, "to sum it up in a single word, I would say 'Efficiency'. . . . That has been our gospel, and the keynote of our administration." It was certainly to be the keynote of his period of office; and no one—the British administrators below him or the newly articulate Indian middle class—was to be allowed to tamper with the grand design.

The India that Curzon arrived in at the end of 1898 seemed calm and secure. Since the end of the Sepoy Revolt of 1857, there had been a long period of internal peace. The British felt safe, and Indians had little doubt of the permanency of the British connexion. There had continued to grow, however, an increasingly vocal Indian middle class, educated in the British tradition and more and more desirous of expressing its sense of equality with the foreigners who ruled India. In 1885, with the support of the government, the Indian National Congress had been established by an Englishman, A. O. Hume. Its members were moderates who saw themselves not as revolutionaries but as playing the same role as that typically British institution, a "loyal opposition"—that of pressing for reforms and, perhaps, one day changing the government from within. The Congress, which the

British had looked upon as a safety valve for the loquacity of the Indian intellectual, a talking-shop productive of nothing but hot air, had already changed by the time of Curzon's arrival. The undercurrents of extremism were now rising to the surface. Curzon, however, preferred to ignore them: "My own belief", he wrote to the Secretary of State for India in 1900, "is that Congress is toppling to its fall, and one of my great ambitions while in India is to assist it to a peaceful demise". It is an irony, certainly in terms of Curzon's beliefs a tragic irony, that two of his administrative acts were to give Indian nationalism a new direction.

Despite all this, British power in 1899, though not entirely unquestioned, was still supreme. Curzon, nevertheless, believed that the administration needed a drastic overhaul. The system was too slow and cumbersome, loaded with useless routine. It reminded him of an elephant, he said, "very stately, very powerful, with a high standard of intelligence but with a regal slowness in its gait". This was the challenge, and he met it head on, with characteristic industry and attention to detail. He must oversee everything; everything new must be initiated by him. "It is no good", he wrote, "trusting a human being to do a thing for you. Do everything yourself." As trust of subordinates and the consequent delegation of power was the basis of Indian administration, the Curzon principle taken to its logical conclusion would quickly have destroyed the whole fabric of British rule in India. The task was too great even for Curzon: but he was able to bring about considerable reforms, many of which were genuine improvements. Unfortunately, he carried them through without finesse or respect for other people's feelings. By his actions, he slowly antagonised everyone, except the mass of the people to whom the Viceroy's industry, wit, and magnificence were meaningless. But the "patient, humble, silent millions", whose interests Curzon believed he served, were no danger to British rule because they *were* silent and humble. Nor, fundamentally, were his own countrymen of the Indian Civil Service who suffered from his reforming zeal. It was the new Indian middle classes who were to be pushed by two of his reforms into a new understanding of their role in India's future.

Curzon's first attack was upon office delays and lengthy minutes.

> Thousands of pages, [he wrote] occupying hundreds of hours of valuable time are written every year by scores and scores of officers, to the obfuscation of their intellects and the detriment of their official work. . . .

Curzon's substitute was to be the committee of inquiry. Unfortunately, these committees would have to be made up of men with little time to spare from their official duties. India was ruled by the very minimum number of British administrators, who could attend committees only if they left their everyday work undone or delegated it to subordinates. Curzon's new system was certainly not in the interests of the efficiency that he sought to instil.

When Curzon arrived in India, he set himself twelve tasks that he proposed to carry out during his period of office. One of the first to receive his attention was the perennial problem of agriculture. He found the agricultural department extremely inefficient, a sad comment on an administration pledged to protect the interests of the Indian peasant. The land revenue system was far too rigid, and little attempt had been made to solve the problem of rural debt. One of the great achievements of Curzon's period of office was the extension of the principle of protecting cultivators, by the Punjab Land Alienation Act of 1900 and other measures, from eviction for debt. Curzon established, with money given by an American friend, research laboratories and experimental farms. He also set up a committee to plan and initiate a long-term programme of irrigation. In the attack upon debt and the stranglehold of the moneylender upon the peasant, Curzon supported the idea of cooperative credit societies, though these societies were not well received by nationalist opinion. Curzon was mainly interested—for he was very much a product of his times—in bringing science to bear upon the problems of Indian agriculture. On the day before he finally left India, in a speech given in Bombay, Curzon answered his own question, "What have we been doing for agriculture? Our real reform," he said, "has been to endeavour for the first time to apply science on a large scale to the study and practice of Indian agriculture." There is little doubt that, despite his attempts to better the physical and moral condition of the Indian peasant, Curzon was right in his estimate.

Curzon was the first Viceroy to consider agriculture as an industry, to see it not only as a source of revenue, but as part of the general economy of the country. He was active, too, in other sectors. Railways were expanded, and a new Railway Board set up to administer and plan development. For commercial and industrial matters, a new

Department of Commerce and Industry was created, and its head made a member of the Viceroy's Council—the cabinet of British India.

Curzon's hand was upon every aspect of the administration. He read everything, probed into every corner, and added to the weight of paper he so despised with incisive and lengthy minutes of his own. Many an Indian Civil Servant must have thought of him as an unsleeping eye, a sort of "Big Brother" continually on the watch. Like the young Gibbon, who felt he *was* the Roman empire, Curzon knew *he* was British India, and he would "swerve neither to the right or the left", caring "nothing for flattery, odium or abuse".

Perhaps the most important of his internal reforms was that of the police. The commission he established produced an indictment of the government that could hardly have made pleasant reading. Training was bad, supervision worse, and the police were "generally regarded as corrupt and oppressive". Reforms were tackled with Curzon's customary energy. Provincial services were established, and a new Criminal Intelligence Department created. Pay was raised; and, in a few years, the strength was increased from 150,000 men to 175,000. Curzon was unable—or possibly unwilling—to secure for the police "the confidence and cordial cooperation of the people" in which it was so sadly lacking and which it still lacks even today. From the British point of view, nevertheless, Curzon's reforms prepared the police for the strain put upon it in the next forty years by political and communal troubles.

It sometimes comes as a surprise, to those who know

little of the history of British India, to learn how small a part of the country was directly administered by the British. Nearly two-fifths of India was divided between over seven hundred princely states, most of whom were in treaty relation with the British Crown. Before the Sepoy Revolt of 1857, Dalhousie had carried out a policy of annexation that had been one of the causes of the mutiny. But, after 1858, believing that they had seen "a few patches of Native government prove breakwaters in the storm which otherwise would have swept over us in one great wave", the British had kept the states as a sort of insurance policy against a further outbreak. Legally, the relations of the princes with the government of India were only through the Viceroy as representative of the Empress of India and her successors, a relationship that was to cause considerable trouble at the time of the transfer of power to independent India in 1947. The Viceroy could, and frequently did, interfere in the internal affairs of the states, if he thought circumstances justified it: but, on the whole, the post-mutiny policy had been one of non-interference. Curzon continued this policy, while giving to it a special slant of his own. As always, he took every opportunity of expressing his views. In 1903, at the installation of a new Nawab of Bahawalpur, the Viceroy pointed out that the princes had become

> figures on a great stage instead of actors in petty parts. . . .
> They are no longer detached appendages of Empire but
> its participators and instruments. They have ceased to
> be the architectural adornments of the Imperial edifice,
> and have become the pillars that help to sustain the main
> roof.

But Curzon was quick to admonish his "partners" when he felt it necessary. Progress, that great Victorian ideal, was not to be hindered by backward native states. The princes' duty was not "passive acceptance of an established place in the Imperial system, but of active and vigorous cooperation in the discharge of its onerous responsibilities". Above all, "they must keep pace with the age". Curzon founded the Imperial Cadet Corps to give military training to the sons of princes; and he insisted that even the least of the native rulers should be treated with courtesy by officials. But, to Curzon, the partnership was hardly one of equals. He continually hectored the princes about their behaviour. Curzon, however, did establish an important point by his continuous stress upon the princes' duties. Although in one sense the princes were not part of British India, their future was implicitly tied to that of those parts of the country under direct administration. Their relations with the Crown were a pleasing fiction that satisfied everybody, but would not be tolerated as an excuse for bad government. Curzon's statement of the position, and its restatement by those who followed him, without doubt prepared the princes for the problems that were to face them when independence came to British India in 1947.

Curzon's concern—and it was a genuine, though rather cold, one—with the material welfare of the Indian people was not purely an expression of the Utilitarian belief that their lot could be improved by government manipulation. "Ignorance", wrote James Mill, the father of Utilitarianism, in his *History of British India* (1819), "is the natural concomitant of poverty . . . but poverty is

E.E.—K*

the effect of bad laws and bad government." Curzon had made it his task to create what he believed to be good government; and his attack upon poverty was part of the package. But he also sought to do something about ignorance; for his imperialism was a combination of the doctrines of utility and a Macaulayan belief in the virtues of Western education. Yet he was not at all narrow-minded about the glories of India's own culture. For the first time since Warren Hastings, there was someone at the head of the government of India who was really interested in Indian art and architecture. He patronised the Asiatic Society of Bengal, of which Hastings had been one of the founders. But his greatest achievement in the cultural field was the creation of a Department of Archaeology, whose function it was to preserve the monuments of Indian art and, by excavations, to discover more of them. Although some work had been done in the past, by Curzon's time "beautiful remains were tumbling into irretrievable ruin simply for the want of a directing hand and a few thousand rupees". Now the bazaars that had grown up around such places as the Taj Mahal were ruthlessly destroyed; the jungle was hacked away from temples, a post-office ejected from a Muslim tomb. In his speech on the Ancient Monuments Act passed in 1904, Curzon put forward his hope that the work he had started would continue and, despite the proposition that the Department should be closed in 1911, it did so until—in the words with which Curzon ended his speech—India could "boast that her memorials are as tenderly prized as they are precious". Curzon's work for Indian archaeology was another, albeit unwitting, contribution to the growing sense of Indian maturity. In its claim for equality against a foreign ruler, a nationalist movement needs some sanction from the past. The English savants of the late eighteenth century, who had discovered the glories of Sanskrit literature, had supplied the foundation. Curzon helped to build the edifice of national pride that was to support Indians in their struggle for freedom.

Most of Curzon's reforms had left the rapidly growing middle class untouched. Westernised Indians could readily accept agricultural reform as a necessity, not for themselves but for the other India in which they were little involved. Education was another matter. Western education had given the middle-class Indians the scaffolding within which they thought and sought to express their ideas. From it, they had acquired their hope in the future; in popular jargon, it was a "status symbol" of great significance. It was over the issue of education that the Indian middle classes began to recognise that Curzon, for all his charm and his apparent willingness to take educated Indians into his confidence, was not really concerned with their feelings or their aspirations—that, in a word, his India was not theirs.

There is no doubt that the educational system was badly in need of reform. The great hopes of Macaulay and others some seventy years before, that English education would filter downwards to produce a new and permanent effect upon India, had not been realised. Higher education, as Curzon put it, had come to mean "a rush of immature striplings to our Indian Universities, not to learn but to earn", to pass examinations, not to acquire a cultured mind. Curzon attacked the problem with his customary efficiency. He began, in 1901, by appointing a conference to ascertain "the trend of authoritative opinion". Unfortunately, all the members were British, and all, except one, government officials. The deliberations were not made public. Curzon's opening speech was a long and pertinent survey of the shortcomings of the system. To remedy them, he wished to change the universities from examining into teaching institutions, to enlarge the scope of secondary education, and to reorganise primary education, whose function he understood to be "the teaching of the masses in the vernacular". The conference, without apparently a dissenting voice—one would hardly expect one from officials—passed a hundred and fifty resolutions, each of which had been drafted by Curzon himself. The whole organisation of the education service was to be revised, and a new director-general appointed to produce some measure of central control over what had previously been left to provincial administrations.

The first reform was in the field of primary education; and, although large grants of public funds were made, the results were disappointing since it failed to arouse any popular enthusiasm. The education offered was strictly secular and had little emotional appeal to those whose world was bounded by religion. One commentator described how "schools grew, and too often disappeared, like mushrooms. Harassed subordinates prepared schemes and went around begging villages to accept schools." But there was little criticism at the time. The weaknesses only became obvious later. The real opposition came over the findings of the university commission that began its inquiry in 1902. This time, there was one Indian amongst its members, a Muslim; and he was later joined by a Hindu. The universities at this time were almost entirely free from government interference. The commission advised drastic changes. The senates were to be reduced in size and to contain a large number of nominated members, including the directors of public instruction. The vice-chancellors were to be appointed by the government, which would also approve all academic appointments. The commission also proposed to reduce the number of students, and to create residential colleges that would have something of the corporate life of Oxford and Cambridge. It also suggested that law classes should be abolished.

The reaction was loud and vocal. Nationalist sentiment at this time tended to polarise around the universities, and government interference here seemed to the teaching profession an attempt to undermine its influence. The cry was raised that the universities would be "practically converted into government departments". Although the Universities Act was passed in 1904, suspicion and resentment rendered it inoperative. The opposition it produced was a forerunner of what was to happen over another reform, that of the partition of Bengal.

During his first period of office, Curzon's attention was not entirely concentrated on internal reform. His vision of India as "the true fulcrum of Asiatic dominion" would not allow him to confine his activities to administration. One problem was both internal and external—that of the North-West Frontier. The British had always feared that Russia had designs upon India; and, as the Tsar's empire extended into Central Asia and reached the borders of

Afghanistan, the danger increased. Two wars had already been fought in an attempt to prevent the Afghans from falling under Russian influence. After the second war in 1879, a strong ruler sat in Kabul, whose main aim was to keep his kingdom intact; and he found that one way of diverting Britain's attention was to encourage intrigue among the Muslim tribes of the area that bordered British India. Until 1893, there was, in fact, no precise border. There was a line where direct administration stopped: but between this and Afghanistan there existed a sort of no-man's-land of tribal territory, in which some of the tribes were said to be British and some Afghan, although none of them was subject to the authority of either power. The tribes often raided the settled areas on the frontier, and attempts at suppression had cost a great deal of money and had involved the mounting of large-scale military operations. The problem, basically, was how to produce a cheap and efficient way of keeping the tribes in order, how to answer violence quickly and decisively.

As far as Afghanistan was concerned, Curzon believed that under strong rule she would be concerned with keeping her independence, and the less interference from India the better. Russia, in any case, since its frontier with Afghanistan had been settled in 1887, now seemed to be looking to the Far East for its next phase of expansion. But the frontier, Afghanistan, and Russia were all aspects of one strategic problem.

When Curzon arrived in 1899, the frontier was still disturbed after the great uprising of 1897, which had been the tribal answer to British attempts to extend formal administration to the tribal areas, attempts that had led to demarcation of the frontier with Afghanistan—the Durand Line—in 1893. Some fifteen thousand troops were still engaged in military activity in the tribal areas. Curzon's policy was, he declared, "withdrawal of British forces from advanced positions, employment of tribal forces in defence of tribal country, concentration of British forces in British territory as a safeguard and a support, importance of communications in the rear". He gradually withdrew the troops and replaced them with tribal levies under British officers, built strategic railways and concentrated mobile columns at bases like Peshawar and Kohat. The aim was to keep the peace, while allowing the tribes to rule themselves so long as they behaved.

Linked with this policy was the creation of the North-West Frontier Province. Until Curzon's time, the frontier had been administered by the Punjab, and its government had found it difficult to handle a settled province with an unsettled border. The new creation included all the trans-Indus territory, except the settled district of Dera Ghazi Khan in the south, and stretched as far as the Afghan boundary. About a third of the area was directly administered, leaving some twenty-five thousand square miles to semi-independent tribesmen. These civil and military reforms brought comparative peace and considerable economy. During his seven years of office, Curzon spent on military operations along the frontier only £248,000 as against £4,584,000 expended between 1894 and 1898. Decisions could also be made more quickly, as the new province was ruled by a chief commissioner directly responsible to the Viceroy. The new reforms did not solve the "frontier problem": but, apart from three small campaigns, the frontier was quiet until the outbreak of war in Europe in 1914.

To the west, Curzon dealt decisively with the problem of Persia and the Gulf. Russia was active in northern Persia, and France and Germany were interested in the south. The home government declared in 1903 that it would regard "the establishment of a naval base or a fortified post in the Persian Gulf as a very great menace to British interests and we should certainly resist it by all means at our disposal". With a display of British sea-power in the Gulf and the increase of Britain's influence by the establishment of consulates and trade agencies, Curzon helped to re-assert her supremacy. An official tour by Curzon in 1903 of Persian and Arabian waters, characterised by a show of naval strength and viceregal pomp, was a further demonstration of Britain's determination to maintain her position in the Gulf. After 1903, little attempt was made to contest it.

The North-West Frontier and Persia were two of Curzon's more successful achievements. In Tibet, the results of the last old-fashioned imperial gesture by the British in Asia were not so satisfying. For two hundred years Tibet, that strange theocracy ruled by an incarnate Buddha, the Dalai Lama, had accepted Chinese suzerainty. Attempts by the British to open trade and political relations had been unsuccessful, although, after the demarcation of the Indo-Tibetan frontier in 1890, a trade convention had been made. Chinese power was in decline, however, and a new Dalai Lama sought to achieve independence. He did this by looking to Russia for help, through a Russian Buddhist monk named Dorjieff. This was too much for Curzon; and, in 1902, he pressed the home government to force a mission on Tibet, which it was unwilling to do, although it finally permitted him to send a mission to open negotiations in the summer of 1903. Troops under Colonel Younghusband advanced fifteen miles inside Tibetan territory, and the Tibetans, refusing to negotiate, gathered together their pitifully medieval army. Again under pressure from Curzon, the home government permitted an advance to Gyantse. After a "battle" at Guru in March 1904, in which six hundred virtually unarmed Tibetans were killed, Younghusband marched on Lhasa, which he captured in August. The harsh terms imposed by Younghusband were rejected by the home government; and the only positive results of the expedition were the stationing of an Indian trade mission at Gyantse and the subsequent re-imposition of Chinese authority. From Curzon's personal point of view, the Tibetan affair was a particular disaster. The white hope of the imperialists had forced his way upon the home authorities, defied their instructions, and had not even produced success as an excuse. Faith in his judgment declined; and, at the time of the dispute with Kitchener, this probably weighed against him.

By 1904, Curzon's first period of office had come to an end. Despite the Tibetan débâcle, it had been a successful one. Although he had antagonised nationalist opinion with his schemes for education, there was no doubt that Indians still respected his vigour and dynamism. In England, too, in spite of some official doubts, he still seemed to embody the vitality of the "unexhausted purpose". The pomp and circumstance and the imperial

incantations of the Delhi Durbar of 1903, at which
Edward VII had been proclaimed Emperor of India,
were to the British what they were to Curzon, an
"overwhelming display of unity and patriotism". Amid
general approval, Curzon was re-appointed for a second
term and returned to India in the autumn of 1904. Now,
however, he was to face bitter disillusion. Everything he
did seemed to go wrong.

Two problems faced him on his return—the administration of Bengal, and army reform. Bengal had always
presented administrative difficulties, not the least of which
was the presence in Calcutta of both the Viceroy and the
Lieutenant-Governor of the province. By 1900, Bengal
had a population of about seventy-eight millions. The
western half of the province, where communications were
good, was prosperous and its people mainly Hindu. East
Bengal, neglected and backward, was predominantly
Muslim. Several schemes for dividing Bengal had been
proposed. It remained to Curzon to put one of them into
practice. The method he adopted was to unite Assam and
Chittagong with fifteen districts of Bengal to form a new
province of Eastern Bengal and Assam, having its capital
at Dacca. The proposed division was, from an administrative point of view, highly desirable: but Curzon left
out of his calculations both nationalist feeling, which he
did not believe existed, and Bengali sentiment, for which
he had no sympathy. Curzon did not understand that vast
changes could no longer be carried through without some
consultation with the people they would affect. In Bengal,
there *was* a sense of the Bengali "nation"; and the
"partition" seemed an attack upon it. Nationalists, who

had failed in their protests against the Universities Act and the general indifference of the administration to their opinions, saw in partition an opportunity for an attack upon the government. Curzon ignored their reasoned protests; and these were followed by vast public demonstrations and a boycott of foreign cloth. Moderate and extreme nationalists were united at last; and at the Indian National Congress meeting of 1906 was first heard the demand for "the system of government obtaining in the self-governing British colonies". The partition also inspired Nawab Salimulla of Dacca to found the Muslim League, which supported the division of Bengal. After Curzon had left India, a campaign of terrorism and government repression began; and partition was finally revoked in 1911. From the division of Bengal, and the crystallisation of national sentiment that it produced, can be dated the beginning of the end of British rule in India.

It was not, however, upon the rock of partition that Curzon's ship was to break, but upon a matter that hardly affected the welfare of India. Curzon had been just as anxious to initiate reforms in the administration of the army in India as he had been to change the civil side of government. To assist him he had asked for, and received in 1902, the appointment of Lord Kitchener, fresh from his triumphs in the South African war. At first, these two masterful men had worked well together: but, on his return to India in 1904, Curzon found his commander-in-chief demanding the abolition of the military member of the Viceroy's council. The military member was a soldier of high rank who acted as the Viceroy's adviser. It was a convenient arrangement; for the C-in-C. was often away from headquarters, and the Viceroy had on hand the opinion of a soldier. Kitchener resented this dual control and wished to be supreme in his own department. Kitchener, whose arrogance was not dissimilar to Curzon's, was not prepared to tolerate a situation in which his proposals, as executive head of the army, were "critcized from the military point of view by the Military Member of Council who must necessarily be both junior in rank and inferior in military experience to the Commander-in-Chief".

Curzon's opinion that a change would mean a decrease in the authority of the civil power was supported by the other members of his Council. But the final decision lay with the home government; and its attempt to effect a compromise was unsatisfactory to either side. In the belief that he was indispensable, Curzon tendered his resignation, which, to his great surprise, was finally accepted in August 1905. The Kitchener reforms were, in fact, carried out, but were abandoned after the strains of the First World War had shown how serious were their defects.

The acceptance of his resignation was a bitter blow to Curzon, and one from which he never fully recovered. But his achievement has a secure place in history. He pushed India into the twentieth century, and gave her an administration that was, in great measure, to survive the shock of independence. There is no doubt that he loved India and sought, within his rigid concept of paternal duty and responsibility, to do something concrete for the mass of her people. He could not see that fatherliness was not enough, that the Indian middle classes were not just the material beneficiaries of British rule, but the legatees of its fundamental principle that all men had the right to rule themselves. He created a gap between the British government and those whom he thought were tied to it by bonds of self-interest that was never closed. Ironically, he was one of the architects of India's independence. Looking back, we can see, too, the irony that lay in the words of his last speech before quitting India. In his work, he said, he had had no other aim than to leave ". . . a sense of manliness or moral dignity, a spring of patriotism, a dawn of intellectual enlightenment or a stirring of duty where it did not before exist". He achieved his aim, although hardly in the way he had intended.

A GENERAL NOTE ON BIBLIOGRAPHY

Historians have written about the expansion of Europe most prolifically, and any guide even to the secondary literature can only be arbitrarily selective. Readers who wish to begin with the earliest stages might turn to J. H. PARRY, *The Age of Reconnaissance*, London, 1963. The same author has written a good account of *The Spanish Sea-borne Empire*, London, 1966. C. R. BOXER has a volume in the same series on *The Dutch Sea-borne Empire*, London, 1966, and has also written widely on early Portugese expansion; his *Salvador de Sà and the Struggle for Brazil and Angola, 1602-86*, London, 1952, illuminates a wide sweep of Portugese expansion. For the contemporary Portuguese empire, the best general survey is still JAMES DUFFY, *Portuguese Africa*, Cambridge, Mass., 1959.

Students seeking a guide to historical research published or in progress should consult the volume by FREDERIC MAURO in the *Nouvelle Clio* series, *L'Expansion européenne, 1600-1870*, Paris, 1964; although it is unsatisfactory in its coverage of work in the English-speaking world.

There is still no good account of French colonial expansion; the least unsatisfactory introductions are probably the works of GEORGES HARDY, such as *Histoire Sociale de la Colonisation française*, Paris, 1953, or in English the two volumes of H. I. PRIESTLEY, *France Overseas*, New York, 1938, 1939. HENRI BRUNSCHWIG has a provocative essay on the expansion of the Third Republic, translated into English as *French Colonialism*, London, 1966. JOHN D. HARGREAVES, *West Africa: The Former French States*, Englewood Cliffs, N.J., 1967, deals with one important area of French influence.

On the German empire MARY E. TOWNSEND, *The Rise and Fall of Germany's Colonial Empire*, New York, 1930, reprinted 1966, is no longer satisfactory, but apart from HENRI BRUNSCHWIG, *L'expansion coloniale allemande de xve siècle à nos jours*, Paris, 1957, there is no general survey to replace it. See however the symposium to be published by Yale University Press on *Britain and Germany in Africa*, edited by PROSSER GIFFORD and WILLIAM ROGER LOUIS.

The best introduction to the rather unusual record of Belgian imperialism may be found in two volumes sponsored by the Institute of Race Relations; RUTH SLADE, *King Leopold's Congo*, London, 1962, and ROGER ANSTEY, *King Leopold's Legacy*, London, 1956.

For the overland expansion of Russia it is probably best to consult the relevant portions of HUGH SETON-WATSON, *The Russian Empire 1801-1917*, Oxford, 1967.

The basic work of reference on formal British expansion is still the eight weighty volumes of *The Cambridge History of the British Empire*, published between 1929 and 1959. A major study, of great influence despite its apparently discursive form, is SIR W. KEITH HANCOCK's *Survey of British Commonwealth Affairs*, 2 vols. in 3, London, 1937-42. Another major enterprise is VINCENT T. HARLOW's *The Founding of the Second British Empire, 1763-93*, 2 vols., London, 1952, 1964. Those wishing further guidance should consult *The Historiography of the British Empire-Commonwealth*, edited by ROBIN WINKS, Durham, N.C., 1966. Two differing appraisals of Britain's imperial experience are KENNETH ROBINSON's Reid Lectures on *The Dilemmas of Trusteeship*, London, 1965, and JOHN STRACHEY, *The End of Empire*, London, 1959.

The fierce debate which is still raging about the nature of the late nineteenth-century imperialism deserves a bibliographical study to itself. Several attempts have been made to illustrate it through historical anthologies, of which the latest and most coherent is D. K. FIELDHOUSE, *The Theory of Capitalist Imperialism*, London, 1967. Of recent substantive contributions, R. ROBINSON and J. GALLAGHER, *Africa and the Victorians*, London, 1961, has been the most influential.

The tendency mentioned in the introductory essay to rewrite history from the point of view of the colonised peoples rather than that of the expanding Europeans can most readily be illustrated by African examples. For a brief conspectus, see R. OLIVER and J. D. FAGE, *A Short History of Africa*, Harmondsworth, 1962; for more extended treatment, consult *The Oxford History of East Africa* (2 vols., 1963, 1965; a third is to come) and the forthcoming *History of West Africa*, edited by J. F. ADE

AJAYI and MICHAEL CROWDER. On Asia, K. M. PANNIK-
KAR, *Asia and Western Dominance; A Survey of the
Vasco da Gama epoch of Asian History 1498-1945*,
London, 1953, gives an interesting perspective.

SUGGESTIONS
FOR FURTHER READING

1. Prester John

BARTHOLD, V. -V. *La Decouverte de l'Asie.* Paris 1947.

BEAZLEY, C. R. *Prince Henry the Navigator,* London 1895.

— *The Texts and Versions of John de Plano Carpini and William de Rubruquis.* London (Hakluyt Society) 1903.

— The Dawn of Modern Geography. Vol. II, London (John Murray) 1901; Vol. III, Oxford (Clarendon Press) 1906.

The Book of Ser Marco Polo, 2 vols. Tr. and ed., Sir H. Yule. Revised by H. C. Cordier. London (John Murray) 1903.

Cathay and the Way Thither, 4 vols. Tr. and ed., Sir H. Yule. Revised by H. C. Cordier. London (Hakluyt Society) 1915.

GROUSSET, R. *L'Empire des Steppes.* Paris 1946.

HOWORTH, SIR H. *History of the Mongols,* Part I. London 1876.

KIMBLE, G. H. T. *Geography in the Middle Ages.* London (Methuen) 1938.

LETTS, M. *Sir John Mandeville: The Man and his Book.* London (Batchworth Press) 1949.

MIGANA, A. "The Early Spread of Christianity in Central Asia and the Far East", *Bulletin of John Rylands Library,* Manchester, Vol. 9 (1925).

MOULE, A. C. *Christians in China Before the Year 1550.* London (Society for Promoting Christian Knowledge). 1930.

PRESTAGE, E. *The Portuguese Pioneers.* London (A. & C. Black) 1933.

ROCKHILL, W. W. *The Journey of William of Rubruck to the Eastern Parts of the World.* London 1900.

2. Speelman and Indonesia

STAPEL, F. W. *Cornelis Janszoon Speelman.* The Hague 1936.

VAN LEUR, J. C. *Indonesian Trade and Society: Essays in Asian Social and Economic History.* The Hague 1955.

VLEKKE, B. H. M. *Nusantara: A History of the East Indian Archipelago.* Cambridge (Harvard University Press) 1945.

WERTHEIM, W. F. *Indonesian Society in Transition: A Study of Social Change.* The Hague 1956.

3. DILLON AND THE PACIFIC

BEAGLEHOLE, J. C. *The Exploration of the Pacific.* London (A. & C. Black) 1966.

Best South Sea Stories, eds. A. Grove Day and Carl Stroven. London (Souvenir Press) 1964.

BUCK, SIR P. H. *Vikings of the Sunrise.* Christchurch (Whitcombe and Tombs) 1954.

DAVIDSON, J. W. "Peter Dillon", *Australian Dictionary of Biography,* Vol. I. Melbourne (University Press) 1966.

The Journal of William Lockerby, Sandalwood Trader in the Fijian Islands During the Years 1808-1809, ed. Sir Everard im Thurn and L. C. Wharton. London (Hakluyt Society) 1925.

4. TREK AND COUNTER-TREK IN SOUTH AFRICA

DE KIEWIET, C. W. *A History of South Africa, Social and Economic.* Oxford (Clarendon Press) 1941.

GOODFELLOW, C. F. *Great Britain and South African Confederation, 1870-1881.* Cape Town (Oxford University Press) 1966.

MARQUARD, L. *The Story of South Africa.* London (Faber) 1963.

OMER-COOPER, J. D. *The Zulu Aftermath: A Nineteenth-Century Revolution in Bantu Africa.* London (Longmans) 1966.

PATTERSON, S. *The Last Trek: A Study of the Boer People and the Afrikaner Nation.* London (Routledge) 1957.

WALKER, E. A. *A History of Southern Africa.* London (Longmans) 1957.

— *The Great Trek.* London (A. & C. Black) 1960.

5. THE MAHDIA

(a) *Four books which formed the traditional British view of the Mahdia*

CHURCHILL, W. S. *The River War.* London 1899.

SLATIN, R. C. *Fire and Sword in the Sudan.* London 1896.

WINGATE, F. R. *Mahdiism and the Egyptian Sudan.* London 1891.

— *Ten Years' Captivity in the Mahdi's Camp 1882-1892.* London 1892.

(b) *Two modern studies, based largely upon
archival sources, Sudanese and European*

COLLINS, R. O. *The Southern Sudan 1883-1898.* New Haven (Yale University Press) 1962.

HOLT, P. M. *The Mahdist State in the Sudan, 1881-1898.* Oxford (Clarendon Press) 1958.

(c) *Other Aspects*

ALLEN, B. M. *Gordon and the Sudan.* London (Macmillan) 1931.

SANDERSON, G. N. *England, Europe and the Upper Nile, 1882-1899.* Edinburgh (University Press) 1965.

TRIMINGHAM, J. S. *Islam in the Sudan.* London (O.U.P.) 1966.

6. J. T. NORTH AND CHILE

DONALD, M. B. "History of the Chile Nitrate Industry", *Annals of Science*, I (1936), pp. 29-47 and 193-216.

GALDAMES, L. *A History of Chile,* tr. and ed., I. J. Cox. Chapel Hill (University of North Carolina Press) 1941.

HERVEY, M. H. *Dark Days in Chile. An Account of the Revolution of 1891.* London 1891-2.

RIPPY, J. F. *British Investments in Latin America, 1822-1949.* Minneapolis (University of Minnesota Press) 1959.

RUSSELL, W. H. *A Visit to Chile and the Nitrate Fields of Tarapacá.* London 1890.

7. THE VICEROYALTY OF LORD CURZON

CURZON, LORD. *British Government in India: The Story of the Viceroys and Government Houses.* London (Cassell) 1925.

EDWARDES, M. *High Noon of Empire: India Under Curzon.* London (Eyre & Spottiswoode) 1965.

FRASER, L. *India Under Curzon and After.* London (Heinemann) 1911.

Lord Curzon in India: Being a Selection from his Speeches as Viceroy and Governor-General of India, ed. Sir T. Raleigh. London (Macmillan) 1906.

RONALDSHAY, LORD. *Life of Lord Curzon,* 3 vols. London (Ernest Benn) 1928.

STOKES, E. *The English Utilitarians and India.* Oxford (Clarendon Press) 1959. Gives the ideological background to Curzon's imperialism.